D0104379

Touring the Upper East Side

Walks in Five
Historic Districts

Jan 1st, 1996

Dear Janie: (Kítara)

I am enjoying incredible time with you in our neighbourhood of Upper East side, specially 86th street.

Through you, New York has become my city.

A hug and a kiss.

i Happy New Year!

Manuel

Touring the Upper East Side

Walks in Five Historic Districts

Andrew S. Dolkart

New York Landmarks
Conservancy
1995

Copyright © 1995
New York Landmarks Conservancy

Design: The Oliphant Press, New York

Contents

This publication was made possible by a
grant from American Express Company.

Additional funding was provided by
The Greenwall Foundation.

Foreword

American Express Company is pleased to have supported the New York Landmarks Conservancy's guidebook, *Touring the Upper East Side: Walks in Five Historic Districts.* We hope that you will take to the streets of these distinctive neighborhoods, with historian Andrew S. Dolkart's work as your guide. But whether touring or reading, we know that you will enjoy learning more about the history and architecture east of Central Park.

The Upper East Side boasts five of New York City's historic districts — areas officially designated as landmark ensembles. In these districts, Manhattan's street grid is enlivened by a diverse array of great buildings of varied scale and style: mansions and museums, town houses and temples, armories and apartments, churches and clubs, and much much more. These contrasts enliven what is already a vibrant, attractive community in which to live and work, as well as a great place to visit.

American Express shares the Landmarks Conservancy's belief that historic preservation enhances the quality of life in cities for residents and visitors alike. The districts featured in this book prove the point. We urge you to explore them, guidebook in hand. And, enjoy your tour!

Sincerely,

Roger Ballou
President, Travel Services Group, U.S.A.
American Express Company

Acknowledgements

This walking tour guidebook would not have been possible without the assistance of a significant number of people. Without the initiative of Susan Henshaw Jones, the former president of the New York Landmarks Conservancy, this project would never have even begun. Peg Breen, the Conservancy's current president, continued the interest in the successful completion of the project. Conservancy staff member Franny Eberhardt and her successor, Roger Lang, oversaw the project from start to finish. The work undertaken by the staff of the Research Department of the New York City Landmarks Preservation Commission, especially in the preparation of the designation reports for the area's five historic districts, provided a crucial base of information on the area, without which the completion of these walking tours would have been far more difficult. The staff at various libraries and archives aided in the research and choice of photographs; notably at the Avery Library at Columbia University, the New York Public Library, the New-York Historical Society, the Library of Congress, the Museum of the City of New York, and the Municipal Archives. Individuals who extended assistance include Paris R. Baldacci, Mary Beth Betts, Ken Cobb, Anne Coffin, Britt Densmore, Christopher Gray, Patricia McHugh, Philip Norkeliunas, Ellen Washburn Martin, Marjorie Pearson, Susan Tunick, Anne Van Ingen, and Anthony C. Wood. Other people, too numerous to mention, many associated in one way or another with a particular site in the districts, assisted with information about buildings. Special thanks is extended to Elisa Urbanelli, project editor, whose suggestions added greatly to the quality of the final work, and to Abraham Brewster and Ron Gordon of The Oliphant Press whose design brought the text to life.

Introduction

Development of the Upper East Side

To most people, New York's Upper East Side is synony-mous with the homes of the city's economic and social elite. While many of New York's grandest residences are in the area bound by Central Park and the East River between 59th and 96th streets, this is in actuality a neighborhood of great diversity that has attracted a wide range of people and includes a tremendous variety of buildings. The story of the development of the Upper East Side begins in the mid-19th century. Prior to this, very little construction had occurred since most people lived farther downtown and much of the land on the Upper East Side remained in the hands of the city gov-ernment or was divided into country estates. By the 1850s, the appearance of scattered wood-frame houses began to impinge upon the rural character, but most of the area still remained free of organized development, hosting a significant population of indigent squatters residing in shantytowns.

A shantytown located on the rocky land to the east of Fifth Avenue at about 91st Street in 1885

Several forces led to the dramatic changes that occurred on the Upper East Side during the second half

Nos. 13-33 East 81st Street in 1892. Designed by Griffith Thomas in 1878, this was one of many brownstone rows that once lined the streets of the Upper East Side.

of the 19th century. The overriding catalyst for change was the unprecedented increase in New York City's population, as vast numbers of foreign immigrants and American-born migrants flooded into the city. This growth in population resulted in the transformation of open land to the north of Manhattan's settled districts into new neighborhoods. During the 1860s and early 1870s, residential construction was centered south of 59th Street. On the Upper East Side, this was a period of spirited land speculation. A few brownstone rowhouses in the Italianate and Neo-Grec styles were scattered on the blocks between Fourth (renamed Park Avenue in 1888) and Fifth avenues, and some rowhouse and tenement construction occurred to the east, but most of the land remained empty, poised for what appeared to be imminent massive development. Almost all plans, however, collapsed with the Panic of 1873, a severe economic depression lasting until about 1879, that sent land values on Upper East Side plummeting.

The financial recovery of the late 1870s, coupled with the inauguration of the elevated railroads on Third Avenue in 1878 and on Second Avenue in 1880, turned the Upper East Side into a prime location for speculative residential real estate investment. The new housing attracted a large population of working- and middle-class people who commuted to jobs downtown. Virtually the entire neighborhood, save Fifth Avenue, as far north as 86th Street, was built up with residences by the mid-1880s; construction surged up to 96th Street by the early 1890s. Much of the new construction (especially west of Lexington Avenue) took the form of Neo-Grec, Queen Anne, or Romanesque Revival stone or brick and stone rowhouses built by speculators for sale to the middle class. Often these rowhouses were purchased by business and professional people, many of whom were successful immigrants or second generation residents of German, German-Jewish, or Irish heritage. Households were often rather large, with extended families and many servants; the servants were generally recent immigrants from Ireland or Germany. Farther to the east, the presence of the noisy and dirty elevated lines created less desirable areas where tenements were erected to house large numbers of working people. A few small rowhouses also appeared here, including those in the Henderson Place Historic District.

Prior to about 1890, most of the city's wealthiest residents were living south of 59th Street in mansions and rowhouses on or near Fifth Avenue. Since Fifth Avenue, adjacent to Central Park, was not yet considered a prestigious residential address, the expensive plots opposite the park remained vacant; this park frontage was simply too expensive for development of middle-class housing. A few large homes were built on this section of Fifth Avenue during the 1880s, but they were the exception. A history of the area written in 1898 noted that "there was, indeed, for a time a hesitancy on the part of the wealthier classes to occupy Fifth avenue facing the park,...but within the last six years the step northward has been positively taken." So rapid was this transformation that by 1915 palatial mansions filled most of the avenue frontage as far north as 96th Street.

With the arrival of the "wealthier classes" on Fifth Avenue, the character of the adjacent side streets changed. A substantial number of the rowhouses were demolished and replaced by new, more elegant resi-

*Fifth Avenue, north
from the Astor Houses
(Richard Morris
Hunt, 1891-96) at
65th Street in the late
1890s*

dences. Many others had their outdated facades replaced
by more stylish fronts — interiors were, of course, also
brought up to the latest standards. Further residential
construction followed the electrification and covering of
the New York Central Railroad's tracks along Park
Avenue early in the 20th century. This action eliminated
the nuisance conditions that had suppressed land values
on that thoroughfare. Suddenly, this wide boulevard and
its adjoining side streets were transformed into a prime
location for new residences. Most of the Upper East
Side's new mansions and townhouses were erected, not
by speculators, but by individuals who commissioned
custom-designed homes for their own use, often from
America's most prestigious architects. Even those houses
erected at the turn of the century by speculative developers bore, as critic Herbert Croly wrote in 1903, "the dis-
tinction of an individual design."

Like those of their middle-class predecessors in the
neighborhood, the households of the wealthy were often
quite large. Most of the area's new residents employed a

12

significant number of servants. There were many Irish maids residing in the neighborhood's new houses, but there were also many servants from other European countries. The wealthiest households often employed English, Swedish, or Norwegian immigrants, apparently reflecting an ethnic hierarchy among domestic employees, with Irish Catholics at the bottom and Protestant English and Scandinavians at the top.

The construction of new housing was accompanied by that of institutional buildings such as churches, synagogues, clubs, schools, and museums which served the social and spiritual needs of the new residents. With the influx of wealthy people, money was available for especially impressive religious buildings, such as Temple Emanu-El and the Church of the Heavenly Rest, and magnificent clubs, such as the Metropolitan, Knickerbocker, and Colony. The Metropolitan Museum of Art, one of New York's preeminent cultural institutions, undertook a major expansion as the Upper East Side was becoming an elite residential neighborhood, turning its back on Central Park, and creating a monumental architectural ensemble on Fifth Avenue that echoed the grandeur of nearby residences.

The era of great mansion and townhouse construction was relatively short lived; almost all of the single-family homes were erected between the late 1890s and about 1915. Rapidly rising land values, the introduction of the income tax in 1913, and the decline in the number of immigrants available for employment as servants, made these houses too expensive for all but the wealthiest. In addition, apartment houses began to be erected with all of the amenities expected in a high-class single-family home, but without the burdens associated with the daily maintenance of a house. Luxury apartment buildings appeared on the Upper East Side in the first decade of the 20th century when several were erected on Madison Avenue. The earliest of the luxurious Fifth Avenue apartments was McKim, Mead & White's No. 998 of 1910-12, built on the corner of 81st Street. At the time this building was erected, the concept of a tall building housing many families under a single roof was anathema to

Fifth Avenue, looking north from East 91st Street. The apartment houses were erected between 1921 and 1928.

many of the city's elite Fifth Avenue residents. As the *Real Estate Record* noted in 1912, "the mere thought of such a possibility struck horror in the hearts of the residents of that thoroughfare." But 998, with its Italian Renaissance palazzo form and sumptuous interior appointments soon won converts among the city's social leaders and it became the prototype for the many luxury apartments that would soon rise in the neighborhood.

Even during the second and third decades of the century, as the rate of apartment house construction rapidly increased, a few new single-family homes were built, especially in Carnegie Hill. Many affluent New Yorkers who did not wish to reside in an apartment but could no longer afford a townhouse near Central Park moved farther east, purchasing old rowhouses and radically remodeling them to meet contemporary standards of taste and convenience. This happened, for example, on the streets of the Treadwell Farm Historic District where

Tall buildings are just beginning to replace the mansions north of 59th Street in this expansive photograph of c.1920. Grand Army Plaza had only recently been completed; note the columns (now lost) that marked the corners of the lawns and the young tress that outlined the formal plan. In the right foreground are the original Savoy (Ralph S. Townsend, 1890-92), and Netherland (W.H. Hume & Sons, 1890-93) hotels which would soon be replaced by more modern establishments.

most of the 1860s and 1870s rowhouses were redesigned between 1919 and 1922.

Very little development occurred on the Upper East
Side during the Depression and World War II. After the
war, several new apartment buildings, often banal
white-brick boxes, were erected. Many of the neighborhood's institutions expanded and others, such as the
Whitney and Guggenheim museums, arrived in the area
and erected spectacular new buildings. The Upper East
Side continues to be one of the most distinguished
neighborhoods of New York City, one where historic
preservation now plays an important role. In fact, several
significant early preservation battles were fought in this
neighborhood. For example, the loss of the Brokaw
Houses on Fifth Avenue and East 79th Street in 1964 was
one of the catalysts for the creation of the Landmarks
Preservation Commission and the Marquesa de Cuevas's
heroic eleventh hour rescue of the Park Avenue Houses
in 1965 saved one of New York's most beautiful blocks.
The designation of the area's five historic districts has
ensured that the historic character of the Upper East Side
will continue to delight generations of New Yorkers and
the many visitors who find the area's streets, shops, and
museums to be among New York City's greatest trea-
sures.

On September 26,
1964, demonstrators
protested the impend-
ing demolition of the
Brokaw Houses.

Architectural Styles on the Upper East Side

As would be expected in an area that developed and redeveloped over a period of many decades, and that was home to people of varied social status and income, the architecture of the Upper East Side is extremely heterogeneous. The buildings in the neighborhood's five historic districts — Upper East Side, Metropolitan Museum of Art, Carnegie Hill, Treadwell Farm, and Henderson Place — successfully illustrate changing stylistic tastes in America beginning in the 1860s. The era between the late 1870s and early decades of the 20th century, when most of the buildings in the historic districts were erected, was a period of enormous flux in the architectural world. The styles and trends that had the greatest impact on the Upper East Side's historic districts are briefly described in this introduction.

Almost all of the early construction on the Upper East Side took the form of rows of narrow houses erected by speculative builders for sale to the middle class. In the late 1860s and early 1870s, the style most popular for these rowhouses was the **Italianate,** with its ubiquitous chocolate-colored brownstone facing. These houses are not copies of Italian Renaissance buildings, rather, their massing and detail are loosely based on Renaissance forms. The flat-roofed rowhouses are composed in a horizontal manner, with a rhythmic repetition of window openings, each generally surrounded by a three-dimensional frame. They commonly have rusticated bases (i.e. blocks of stone separated by deep grooves) and high stoops leading to parlor-level entrances. The characteristic arched entry with double doors is generally recessed within a deep sculptural surround topped by a pediment that is supported on curving brackets often ornamented with rich foliate detail. Each house is crowned by a pressed, galvanized-iron cornice with similar curving brackets.

In the late 1870s, the ornament used on brownstone-fronted rowhouses changed with the advent of the Neo-

Grec style. **Neo-Grec** rowhouses are identical in form and massing to their Italianate predecessors, but the lush curving ornament is supplanted by angular, stylized forms and incised detail. Italianate and Neo-Grec rowhouses are found throughout the East Side's historic districts. Examples are illustrated on pages 10, 56, 104, and 105.

By the early 1880s, as the seemingly endless rows of brownstone houses began to be looked on with disfavor by architects, builders, and homeowners, a new freedom appeared in residential design. The first buildings to evince the new trend were designed in the **Queen Anne** style. Popularized in England in the 1860s by the architect Richard Norman Shaw and his followers and introduced in America in the late 1870s, Queen Anne housefronts combine features from a variety of historical styles, including Classical, Gothic, Renaissance, Dutch, and Japanese. The designs also exploit the properties of several materials. Most buildings are clad in red brick and are trimmed with rough and smooth stone, terra cotta, wood and slate shingles, and iron. Quirky rooflines and rich textural contrasts create whimsical facades. While never as common on the East Side as on the West Side, some of Manhattan's finest Queen Anne rowhouses are found on East 95th Street in the Carnegie Hill Historic District (CH21) and within the Henderson Place Historic District (illustrated on pages 110 and 113).

Also popular during the 1880s and early 1890s was the **Romanesque Revival,** first used by the great American architect Henry Hobson Richardson, and identified by the prevalence of heavy round-arched openings and by the use of massive rough-stone blocks that contrast with smooth stone, brick, and terra-cotta elements. Other defining features include asymmetrical massing, stylized Byzantine carving, and high L-shaped stoops. Romanesque Revival rowhouses are rare on the Upper East Side, but several examples can be found in the Carnegie Hill Historic District (CH16; see page 90).

The course of American architecture changed dramatically in the 1890s, especially following the World's Columbian Exposition held in Chicago in 1893. This world's fair popularized monumental European architecture as a model for American design. The asymmetry, textural richness, and use of earth-tone materials seen on Queen Anne and Romanesque Revival buildings were replaced by a renewed interest in the symmetry and balance of classical and renaissance architecture. Most of the new buildings were clad in light-colored stone or brick, with limestone as the most popular material. It was just at this time that the Upper East Side experienced a major population shift as the wealthy began to displace the earlier middle-class residents. The designs of the grand homes and institutions erected for the wealthy were derived from either contemporary French architecture or from a variety of historical styles. These sophisticated, historically-inspired residences reflect the belief, popular in educated circles at the time, that America was the natural inheritor of European civilization and the artistic traditions of European culture.

Many of the new mansions and townhouses were designed in the **Beaux-Arts** style, named for the Ecole des Beaux-Arts in Paris where American architects increasingly went to receive formal training. These houses resemble those erected in French cities during the final decades of the 19th century. The finest Beaux-Arts townhouses, such as the Fabbri (UES6) and Wilson (UES 20) houses in the Upper East Side Historic District (see pages 29 and 38), are exuberant structures with a plasticity in their massing accentuated by the use of undulating balconies, tall chimneys, and impressive mansard roofs. The facades are often extremely ornate, with a rich incrustation of sculptural detail. The most prominent carved ornamental feature is the cartouche, a three-dimensional shield-like form often embellished with luxuriant carving.

Other houses from the turn of the century were designed in European revival modes, borrowing forms from the architecture of various periods in the history of Italian, French, or English design. While walking these tours, one will encounter buildings in the François I style, recalling the early 16th-century châteaux of the Loire Valley (MM8 and CH27; see pages 67 and 98); in various French 18th-century modes found on the urban houses of Paris and other cities (CH22b; see page 94); in the late 16th- and early 17th-century style of English Elizabethan and Jacobean country houses (UES33; see page 48); in the style of London's 18th- and early 19th-century Georgian and Regency townhouses (CH17), and in many other styles.

The most popular revival style on the Upper East Side is the **Italian Renaissance Revival.** Buildings inspired by the Italian Renaissance are closely modeled on the palazzi built in Florence, Rome, and other Italian cities during the 15th and 16th centuries. The New York buildings often borrow features from particular architectural sources. This contrasts with the earlier Italianate style rowhouses which incorporated generic details with less specific Renaissance origins. The Italian Renaissance Revival style was introduced in New York by McKim, Mead & White at the Villard Houses of 1883-85, located on Madison Avenue between 50th and 51st streets. Although some of the finest examples on the Upper East Side were designed by this firm, including the Pulitzer House (UES42; see page 54), the apartment building at 998 Fifth Avenue (MM13), and the Metropolitan Club (UES3), many other architects designed major works in the style (see pages 52 and 59). Like their Renaissance models, these New York buildings are monumental structures, almost always designed with a tripartite horizontal massing, sculptural window surrounds, and a crowning cornice.

During this period, American architects looked not only to the European past, but also to early American architecture, reviving 18th- and early 19th-century "Colonial" design. McKim, Mead & White also inaugurated this style in New York and was responsible for some of the finest early examples on the Upper East Side (UES29; see page 46). It was, however, the succeeding generation of architects, most significantly the firm of Delano & Aldrich, working in the second and third decades of the 20th century, who are most closely associated with this style (CH19; see page 92). This **Colonial Revival** approach was employed on a wide range of buildings; within the historic districts are townhouses (CH19), clubs (UES4), apartment buildings (CH6; see page 81), banks (UES16), and a church (UES14). These buildings are invariably clad in brick laid in traditional Flemish bond (i.e. alternating long and short bricks). Their extremely flat facades are highlighted by elegant detail carved in white marble or limestone, and often further ornamented with delicate wrought-iron railings and balconies.

By the 1920s only a few New Yorkers could afford the cost of erecting or even maintaining a single-family home on the Upper East Side; by then, most of the area's wealthy residents lived in luxury apartment houses, generally designed in the Italian Renaissance and Colonial Revival modes. Some of those who wished to remain in single-family homes purchased the old brownstone houses of the 1860s and 1870s, which the magazine *Architecture* called a "blight... handed down to the present generation of architects as an heirloom," intending to redesign these buildings. Interiors were modernized and the facades were stripped of their "offending" brownstone stoops and sculpted detail. Streetfronts were coated with smooth stucco subtly ornamented with decorative highlights, creating a new residential aesthetic; such changes are best seen in the Treadwell Farm Historic District (see page 104).

Although almost all of the buildings in the five historic districts were erected before 1930, the districts contain a few important modern structures, including two early houses designed by pioneering Modernist William Lescaze (UES34 and 44; see page 56) and several significant Modern museums, notably Frank Lloyd Wright's Guggenheim (CH5) and Marcel Breuer's Whitney (UES45). Much of the work that has occurred in the districts in recent years has entailed the restoration of earlier buildings, ensuring that the architecture of the Upper East Side's historic districts will continue to be one of New York City's greatest assets.

A Note on the Tours

This guide consists of five walking tours, each examining an Upper East Side historic district designated by the New York City Landmarks Preservation Commission. The architecture and development of the Upper East Side is the main thrust of these walks and they include discussions of many of the most interesting and most beautiful buildings in New York City. However, walkers (and armchair readers) will find more than simple architectural description in the entries. Architecture does not exist in a void, but reflects larger social and cultural trends. Thus, among other issues, the tours highlight development patterns, architectural styles, and notable architects; questions are broached regarding the symbolism or meaning of various design fashions; and the people who lived their lives in these houses are examined.

Each tour is written as a complete unit, but several tours can be linked together. Alternatively, a walker can pause in the midst of a tour to visit a museum or gallery, shop in the neighborhood's elegant stores, grab a meal, or simply relax with a cappuccino, picking up the tour hours or days later. There are so many fascinating buildings within the Upper East Side's historic districts that it is impossible to include all of them on walking tours of reasonable length. We apologize if your favorite building has been excluded.

While taking the tours there are a few things you should keep in mind. When looking at a building, you may find that you can see more if you stand on the opposite side of the street where a comprehensive view of a structure and its setting can be had. You may wish, however, to get up close to a building to examine details. Buildings have generally been named for their original owner or use; current names are provided where applicable. The architect and building indices should aid in finding a particular structure. Remember that most of the buildings on the tour are not open to the public.

Tour I: The Upper East Side Historic District

Introduction

The Upper East Side Historic District, designated in 1981, is one of New York City's largest landmark districts, stretching along Fifth Avenue from 59th Street to 78th Street and as far east, at certain points, as Third Avenue. This is an area synonymous with wealth and social standing, for since the turn of the century, it has housed many of the city's most affluent people. The Upper East Side is, however, no stuffy backwater, but one of the most vibrant neighborhoods of New York. The history of development in this district is representative of the broad trends that created today's Upper East Side. The open land was developed into a bustling middle-class residential community in the decades following the Civil War, only to be almost totally transformed at the turn of the century into a neighborhood of mansions and townhouses that welcomed many of the country's wealthiest households. In the 20th century, as living conditions changed, many of these were replaced by luxury apartment buildings. Today, the district contains a rich mixture of modest brownstone rowhouses, opulent townhouses and mansions, and imposing apartment buildings, including many of the finest examples of urban residential architecture in America.

Tour

UES1 Grand Army Plaza

(Carrère & Hastings, 1913-16). Grand Army Plaza is the magnificent gateway to the Upper East Side (see page 15). As part of their design for Central Park in the 1850s, Frederick Law Olmsted and Calvert Vaux laid out a simple plaza on Fifth Avenue at 59th Street. By the turn of the century, taste had veered away from Olmsted and Vaux's aesthetic, and the plaza was redesigned as a grand

Begin: General Sherman Monument in Grand Army Plaza, Fifth Avenue north of 59th Street

ceremonial space. Joseph Pulitzer's 1912 bequest of $50,000 for a fountain led to a new design by Carrère & Hastings, who created an urbane elliptical space with formal planting beds and a multi-tiered fountain crowned by Karl Bitter's figure of Pomona, goddess of abundance. Augustus Saint-Gaudens's masterful General Sherman Monument of 1892-1903, which stands on a base designed by Charles McKim, was repositioned to align with the fountain. The plaza, named Grand Army Plaza in 1923, was partially restored in 1988-90. Work included the renewal of the original gilded finish on the Sherman Monument.

UES2a Sherry-Netherland Hotel

781 Fifth Avenue, northeast corner East 59th Street (Schultze & Weaver and Buchman & Kahn, 1926-27) and **UES2b Pierre Hotel,** 795 Fifth Avenue, southeast corner East 61st Street (Schultze & Weaver, 1929-30). These two towered hotels form a visual anchor at the southwest corner of the Upper East Side. Both were designed by Schultze & Weaver, a firm that specialized in hotel work (they were also responsible for the Waldorf-Astoria). Although transient guests were welcome, the hotels were planned primarily as residential establishments with luxury suites. The defining visual element of the Sherry-Netherland, the world's tallest apartment hotel at the time of its completion, is the thin French Gothic pinnacle that rises from a tall tower and provides the building with a distinctive silhouette. In the lobby are a pair of relief panels by Karl Bitter salvaged when the Cornelius Vanderbilt House at Fifth Avenue and 57th Street was demolished in 1925. Also of special interest is the hotel's cast-iron sidewalk clock, one of the few still standing in New York City. The Pierre was founded by restaurateur Charles Pierre and is famed for the understated elegance of its public rooms. At its completion the pseudonymous New Yorker writer "Penthouse," described the Pierre as "a millionaires' Elysium."

Walk to the edge of the Plaza at the southwest corner of Fifth Avenue and 60th Street.

Main Hall of the
Metropolitan Club in
1895.

UES3 Metropolitan Club

1 East 60th Street, northeast corner Fifth Avenue
(McKim, Mead & White, 1891-94). In 1891, J.P. Morgan, William and Cornelius Vanderbilt, and other
wealthy New York gentlemen organized a new club that
would rival the staid Union Club (UES31) which had
recently rejected several of their friends. Named the Metropolitan Club, the new organization commissioned
Stanford White to design a clubhouse on this prime Fifth
Avenue corner. The resulting building is one of the
architectural masterpieces of the "American Renaissance." The beautifully proportioned exterior, faced
with two kinds of white marble and crowned by a copper cornice, resembles the Renaissance palazzi of Italian
cities. The simplicity of the public facades contrasts with
the grandeur of the private interiors. In order to provide
a lounging room overlooking Fifth Avenue, the main
entry was situated on 60th Street. White placed the front
door within a courtyard guarded by a screen of columns
and magnificent French-inspired, wrought-iron gates. A
successful facade restoration was completed in 1991.

UES4 Knickerbocker Club

2 East 62nd Street, southeast corner Fifth Avenue
(Delano & Aldrich, 1913-15). Founded in 1871 as a

Cross Fifth Avenue
and walk down
60th Street to view
the Metropolitan
Club's courtyard.
Before returning to
Fifth Avenue notice the Harmonie
Club (1904-07) at
4 East 60th Street,
one of Stanford
White's less successful designs.
Turn right on Fifth
Avenue and walk
to East 62nd
Street.

reaction to the relaxation of admissions standards at the Union Club (UES31), the Knickerbocker has long been among New York's most exclusive social institutions; in fact the term "Knickerbocker" was coined by Washington Irving to refer to members of the city's socially prominent old families. In 1913 the club purchased this fashionable Fifth Avenue site and commissioned a new building from Delano & Aldrich. This firm often combined historic American Colonial and English Neo-classical forms, creating deceptively simple buildings, of which the Knickerbocker is an early masterpiece. The flat rectilinear wall planes of brick laid in Flemish bond are punctuated by large multi-paned windows and enriched with the subtlest of ornament. A meticulous restoration was completed in 1992.

Turn right onto East 62nd Street.

UES5 Fifth Avenue Synagogue

5 East 62nd Street (Percival Goodman, 1956). Percival Goodman was one of the most respected designers of modern synagogues. This pinkish stone building follows the scale of the nearby townhouses, but its unadorned facade, pierced by elliptical stained-glass windows, sets it apart from its neighbors.

UES6 Ernesto and Edith Fabbri House

(Now Johnson O'Connor Research Foundation), 11 East 62nd Street (Haydel & Shepard, 1898-1900). At the turn of the century, it was customary for members of the Vanderbilt family to present their children with expensive new townhouses as wedding gifts. The widowed Mrs. Elliott F. Shepard, née Margaret Vanderbilt, commissioned this house for her daughter Edith and son-in-law Count Ernesto Fabbri of Italy, hiring her nephew's architectural firm, Haydel & Shepard, to design the building. This obscure firm produced an extraordinary Beaux-Arts style townhouse. The dynamic limestone and brick street facade is animated by the varied shapes of the window openings and is enhanced by exceptionally well-conceived robust ornamentation. Note, in particular, the panels embellished with classically-inspired figures, the three magnificently carved cartouches set

Fabbri House,
c. 1900

between the second and third floors, the deep cornice
with its bold brackets, and the iron balconies incorporat-
ing the letter "F." The Fabbris occupied the house spo-
radically, as the count's work often took the family to
Paris; it was sold in 1912. In 1916, the Fabbris returned
to New York, moving into a new home at 7 East 95th
Street (CH24).

Continue east to
the corner of
Madison and East
62nd Street.

Louis Sherry in 1929

UES7 Louis Sherry

(Now The Limited), 691 Madison Avenue, northeast corner East 62nd Street (McKim, Mead & White, 1928). Louis Sherry was one of New York's leading restaurateurs and caterers. His most famous restaurant was located on Fifth Avenue and 44th Street from 1898 until its closing in 1919 which, Sherry asserted, was caused by "prohibition and war-born Bolshevism" (just what Bolshevism had to do with the closing remains a mystery). An eating establishment with Sherry's name was revived following his death when this stylized Neo-classical building, inspired by contemporary French commercial design, was opened to the public. The large plate-glass windows were planned to draw the attention of passersby to the elaborate displays of gourmet foods sold in what was called the "table luxury shop." Behind the store were a tea room and ice cream parlor and a balcony restaurant. In 1984-85, The Limited clothing chain hired Beyer Blinder Belle to restore McKim, Mead & White's building and construct a rooftop addition. The original building received an award from the Fifth Avenue Association in 1929 and the restoration has won several design and preservation awards.

Cross Madison and continue east on 62nd Street.

UES8 Miss Keller's Day School

(Now Revlon, Inc.), 35 East 62nd Street (George Keller,

1904-05). This rather idiosyncratic Italian Renaissance-inspired building was planned by Hartford architect George Keller for use by his niece's girls school. This was one of the first buildings in New York City with a reinforced concrete frame, thus insuring protection from fire and permitting large, unencumbered open spaces on the interior. After the school closed in 1911, the building served several institutional uses, before its purchase in 1990 for conversion into the headquarters of Revlon. Buttrick White & Burtis undertook a careful restoration of the exterior that included cleaning the facade and replacing some of the terra cotta on the loggia.

UES9 Links Club

36 East 62nd Street (Cross & Cross, 1916-17). The Links, a club for country-club golfers desirous of a city retreat, hired Cross & Cross to reconfigure two rowhouses for their clubhouse. The firm provided an English Georgian-inspired facade of red brick trimmed with a marvelous yellow stone. The design, resembling that of gentlemen's clubs in London, focuses on the projecting central section that is embellished with the club's seal and three female masks. The club's initials intertwine on iron grilles at the basement windows. A critic, writing in *Architectural Record* in 1917, commented that the club was "designed for those who like the effects of quiet breeding, traditional elegance, [and] considered good taste." In other words, the restrained Neo-classicism chosen for the club's public image reflected the elite pedigree of its members.

UES10 Colony Club

564 Park Avenue, northwest corner East 62nd Street (Delano & Aldrich, 1914-16). Founded in 1903, the Colony was the earliest social club organized by and for women. Soon after its founding, the club erected its first building on Madison Avenue in Murray Hill, but within a decade it had outgrown this facility. A Park Avenue site was acquired and Delano & Aldrich, the firm that had recently finished the Knickerbocker Club (UES4), was hired as architect for the Colony's new building. The

Continue east on East 62nd Street, past the handsome medieval-inspired, brick and terra-cotta apartment house at No. 40 (Albert Joseph Bodker, 1910-11), to the corner of Park Avenue. The best view of the next four entries is from the landscaped mall in the middle of the avenue.

*Colony Club gymna-
sium, c. 1916*

design of the brick, marble, and limestone structure is
loosely based on the original Federal Hall on Wall Street,
where George Washington took the oath of office as the
nation's first president. This is not one of Delano &
Aldrich's more elegant works in the Colonial idiom, perhaps because it was nearly impossible to create a well-
proportioned design for a building with the complex
spatial requirements of this club. The beautifully
appointed interior included the lounges, dining rooms,
and bedrooms common to social clubs, but also had a
two-story ballroom, a basement swimming pool and spa
that connected via an express elevator to a gymnasium
on the fifth floor, two squash courts, servants' rooms (in
1925 there were thirteen resident female servants), and
even a kennel where members could check their pets.

UES11 550 Park Avenue

Southwest corner East 62nd Street (J.E.R. Carpenter,
1916-17). Apartment house construction on Park
Avenue began in 1907. Almost all of the apartment
buildings erected over the next two decades were charac-
terized by stone at the base with brick above; a few were
entirely clad in limestone. Most had cornices or distinctive rooftop setbacks, and were embellished with subtle
stone or terra-cotta ornament derived from either Italian
Renaissance or American Colonial design. No. 550 is a
good example of an early Renaissance-inspired Park
Avenue apartment house, albeit one that at 17 stories is

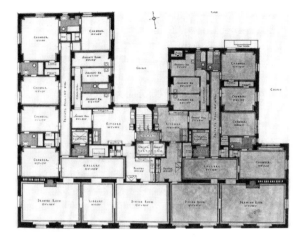

*J.E.R. Carpenter's
beautifully integrated
plan for 550 Park
Avenue*

taller than most of its contemporaries. Architect J.E.R.
Carpenter, a specialist in luxury apartment house design,
is known for providing well-planned units. Built as a
cooperative, the building initially had 32 apartments —
generally one apartment of twelve rooms and one of ten
on each floor. The accompanying plan shows the clear
division, in each apartment, between public rooms for
entertaining, private bedrooms, and servant's quarters.
Among the original residents were the architect and his
wife.

UES12a 563 Park Avenue
Northeast corner East 62nd Street (Walter B. Chambers,
1909-10) and **UES12b 570 Park Avenue,** southwest
corner East 63rd Street (Emery Roth, 1915-16). Although never as popular a stylistic model for luxury
apartment house facades as the Italian Renaissance, the
Colonial Revival was also widely adapted for these buildings. Two especially beautiful examples are visible here.
No. 563, with its arched windows and iron balcony railings, is an early example of the use of the Colonial idiom
for apartment houses. At No. 570 Emery Roth chose a
style that would echo the adjacent Colony Club, even
repeating the club's two-story marble base onto his
building and using expensive red face bricks, laid in a
diaper pattern, for the side and rear walls.

UES13 555 Park Avenue

Southeast corner East 62nd Street (George & Edward Blum, 1912-13). Very few early 20th-century architects attempted to design apartment buildings using non-traditional detail or experimented with stylistically distinct ornamentation. The firm of George & Edward Blum was among the most original designers of the period and their distinctive ornamental vocabulary is evident on No. 555. Here, the traditional tripartite composition of a New York apartment house facade is enlivened by a spectacular use of materials: narrow Roman bricks laid in complex patterns with deeply recessed mortar joints, marble panels, and a unique vocabulary of terra-cotta and iron ornamentation.

Return to the west side of Park Avenue; turn right and walk to 63rd Street.

UES14a Third Church of Christ, Scientist

583 Park Avenue, northeast corner East 63rd Street (Delano & Aldrich, 1922-24) and **UES14b Park Avenue Baptist Church** (now Central Presbyterian Church), 593 Park Avenue, southeast corner East 64th Street (Henry C. Pelton and Allen & Collens, associated architects, 1920-22). There are six churches along the residential portion of Park Avenue, two of which are visible here. Delano & Aldrich's design for the Third Church of Christ, Scientist is a free adaptation of 18th-century Colonial design. Conveying an image of historic America, this was an appropriate stylistic choice for a group with roots in New England. To the north is the Neo-Gothic Park Avenue Baptist Church, erected with funds provided in part by John D. Rockefeller, Jr. An extremely devout man, Rockefeller taught Bible classes in the church basement until 1928 when the congregation sold the building and moved to Riverside Church (also a Rockefeller project).

Turn left onto the north side of East 63rd Street.

UES15 East 63rd Street between Park and Madison Avenues.

In microcosm, this street tells the story of the development that transformed the Upper East Side into a prosperous residential area. All the vacant land on these two blockfronts was built up in the late 1870s and early

34

1880s with middle-class rowhouses, most in the Neo-Grec style; Nos. 43 and 47 (Thom & Wilson, 1882-84), with their brownstone fronts, high stoops, and heavy cornices, survive from this period. During the first three decades of the 20th century many of the old houses were either replaced or had their facades redesigned, most in the popular Colonial and Neo-classical revival styles. An example of this is the house at No. 29 which received a new facade in 1908 designed by Katherine C. Budd, one of the first women to practice architecture in New York. As the neighborhood became more and more exclusive, private clubs appeared, such as the former Hangar Club (Cross & Cross, 1929-30) at No. 36, a close cousin to Cross and Cross' Links Club (UES9), founded by men interested in flying; note the central keystone displaying the winged head of the Roman god Mercury.

By the early 20th century a few tall buildings were appearing on the Upper East Side, especially along Madison Avenue. The Leonori, an apartment hotel at the southeast corner of Madison and 63rd Street (Buchman & Fox, 1901-02), was among the earliest. During the 1910s and 1920s, apartment houses became much more common. Architects such as Emery Roth, who designed the building on the south corner of Park Avenue in 1915, and J.E.R. Carpenter, who was responsible for the 1923 building on the north corner, established successful careers designing this increasingly popular type of residence. Even the side streets were not immune from redevelopment with tall buildings, as is evident at the 17-story Hotel Lowell at No. 28 (Henry S. Churchill, 1925-26), with its spectacular Art Deco pink terra-cotta entrance capped by an octagonal mosaic panel by Bertram Hartman.

UES16 The Bank of New York

Walk to the corner of Madison Avenue.

706 Madison Avenue, southwest corner East 63rd Street (Frank Easton Newman, 1921-22). This handsome structure is one of several Colonial-inspired banks erected on Madison Avenue during the 1920s and early 1930s. The Colonial Revival, with its aura of tradition

*Interior of the Bank of
New York, c.1950*

and stability was an apt choice for bank branches that
catered to affluent people. This is an intimate building,
exuding an exclusivity that the bank's depositors would
have appreciated. The modest scale and quiet domestic-
ity contrast dramatically with the grand public halls of
savings banks then being erected elsewhere in the city
which were designed to attract a wider range of depositors. The New York Life Insurance and Trust Company
commissioned this building, but in 1922, as it was near-
ing completion, that firm merged with the Bank of New
York. The Bank of Manhattan (now Chase Manhattan
Bank) erected a stylistically similar branch in 1932-33
(Morrell Smith, architect), visible one block to the north.

UES17a 690-700 Madison Avenue
at East 62nd Street (J.H. Valentine, 1878-79) and
UES17b 710-718 Madison Avenue at East 63rd Street
(Gage Inslee, 1871-72). Most of the early rowhouses in
the Upper East Side Historic District survive on Madison
Avenue, where the encroachment of commerce early in
the century inhibited the construction of elegant residences. The rhythm of narrow shopfronts projecting
from these old buildings is what lends Madison Avenue
its special character. The Italianate brownstone-fronted
houses at Madison and 63rd Street and the somewhat
later Neo-Grec row at 62nd Street retain much of their
original detail, including carved window enframements,

galvanized-iron cornices, and, at No. 718, an original stoop and arched entrance. The conversion from single-family residences began in the early years of the 20th century and by 1915 about half of the houses in these two rows had stores in the lower floors and apartments above.

UES18 Verona

Cross Madison and turn right. Walk to East 64th Street.

32 East 64th Street, southeast corner Madison Avenue (William E. Mowbray, 1907-08). The builders of the Verona were pioneers in the development of luxury apartment houses on the Upper East Side, for this is one of the earliest grand apartment houses in the neighborhood. The Verona was planned with only twenty apartments (two per floor), each originally consisting of eleven rooms and three baths. As one would expect from a building named the Verona, this is an Italian Renaissance-inspired structure, although the horizontal composition of a three- or four-story Italian palazzo is here expanded vertically to create a ten-story building. The office of architect Jan Pokorny was responsible for a 1987-88 restoration that included extensive work on the magnificent cornice.

UES19 Wildenstein & Co. Gallery

Turn left on East 64th Street.

19 East 64th Street (Horace Trumbauer, 1931-32). By the 1920s, the city's commercial art galleries were following their patrons north. Wildenstein Gallery, founded in Paris in 1875, had opened a New York branch on Fifth Avenue near 52nd Street in 1902. In 1932 the prestigious gallery moved to East 64th Street. Modeled after 18th-century Parisian townhouses, the gallery building conforms to its residential setting; only the display windows hint at its actual use. Here, Wildenstein displayed Old Master paintings in a domestic setting not unlike the homes of many of its clients.

UES20 Marshall Orme and Caroline Astor Wilson House

Continue west on 64th Street.

(Now New India House), 3 East 64th Street (Warren & Wetmore, 1900-03). Warren & Wetmore's finest town-

Wilson House,
c. 1904

Continue to Fifth
Avenue.

house was begun in the year that the nearby Fabbri
(UES6) and Schieffelin (UES23) houses were completed
and, like them, is an important example of Beaux-Arts
design. However, the use of sculptural Beaux-Arts forms
differs markedly from that on its contemporaries. Here, a
relatively unornamented limestone facade is crisply
pierced by arched windows that are deeply recessed
within concave frames. Ornament is used sparingly to
emphasize features such as the entrance and the second-
story windows. The building is crowned by one of the
most beautifully articulated mansard roofs in New York.
The small round windows in the mansard probably provided minimum light and air to the rooms where the
Wilsons' many servants lived. Marshall Orme Wilson
was a banker married to Caroline Schermerhorn Astor,
daughter of William B. Astor, Jr. and Caroline Webster

Schermerhorn Astor ("the Mrs. Astor"). The Indian government has owned the property since 1950.

UES21 Edward and Herminie Berwind House

828 Fifth Avenue (Nathan C. Mellen, 1893-96). Edward Berwind, reputed to have been the largest coal baron in the United States, is probably best known today as the builder of The Elms, one of Newport's grandest mansions. Several years before that summer home was begun, Berwind erected this Fifth Avenue residence, designed by an architect about whom little is known. Mellen produced a somewhat awkward structure reminiscent of the Venetian Renaissance. The glass penthouse was added during conversion to apartments in 1978.

Cross Fifth Avenue. Turn right and walk to East 65th Street.

Presentation drawing for Temple Emanu-El

UES22 Temple Emanu-El

840 Fifth Avenue, northeast corner East 65th Street (Robert D. Kohn, Charles Butler, and Clarence S. Stein, associated architects with Mayers, Murray & Phillip, consultants, 1927-29). Emanu-El, the oldest Reform Jewish congregation in New York and one of the city's most important religious institutions, was founded in 1845. In 1866-68, after occupying two former churches, Emanu-El erected a spectacular Moorish-inspired synagogue on Fifth Avenue and 43rd Street. By the 1920s,

skyscrapers and other commercial buildings surrounded the synagogue and most congregants lived elsewhere — many on the Upper East Side. Thus, in 1926 the congregation announced that it had purchased the twin mansions erected in 1891-95 for Mrs. William B. Astor and her son John Jacob Astor IV on Fifth Avenue at 65th Street (see page 12). This move was somewhat problematic since another reformed synagogue, Congregation Beth-El, was located only a few blocks north. A merger was arranged in 1927 and construction began.

The new Temple Emanu-El was designed with a sanctuary seating 2500, the adjacent Beth-El Chapel, and a tall community house with Sunday school rooms, social halls, and offices. The main synagogue is an impressive limestone structure with bold massing reminiscent of such works by Bertram Goodhue as St. Thomas Episcopal Church. This similarity is not coincidental; one of the main architects, Clarence Stein, had been the chief designer in Goodhue's office, and the consulting architectural firm of Mayers, Murray & Phillip was Goodhue's successor. Although the basic form and massing of the building, as well as the rose window and stylized flying buttresses, are Gothic in inspiration, the exterior detail is loosely Romanesque. The focal point of the Fifth Avenue front is the tall central arch with its richly carved decoration, including symbols of the Twelve Tribes of Israel. The chapel, set back from Fifth Avenue behind a small garden, acts as a transition between the main sanctuary and the apartment house to the north. The austerity of the temple's monochromatic exterior belies the richness of its interior (entrance is through the community house).

Continue north and turn right onto East 66th Street.

UES23 William and Maria Schieffelin House

(Now Lotos Club), 5 East 66th Street (Richard Howland Hunt, 1898-1900). In 1898, Margaret Vanderbilt Shepard commissioned houses for her two daughters — Edith Fabbri and Maria Schieffelin. The Beaux-Arts house built for the Schieffelins is not as successful as Edith Fabbri's (UES6), perhaps because the juxtaposition of white limestone and red brick is jarring and the massive ornamentation appears to overpower the facade. Unquestionably, the building's finest feature is the glorious pair of oak doors with ornate carved moldings and female heads. William Schieffelin was chairman of the board of Schieffelin & Co., a wholesale drug firm established in 1793, and was active in reform politics and efforts to improve conditions for the city's black population; Maria Schieffelin was a major backer of the Y.W.C.A. By 1925, the Schieffelins had moved into an apartment building and the house became the Deutscher Verein (German Club). The Lotos, an arts club founded in 1870, purchased the property in 1946.

Ernest Flagg's elevation drawing for the Scribner House

UES24 Charles and Louise Flagg Scribner House

(Now Permanent Mission of the Republic of Poland to the United Nations), 9 East 66th Street (Ernest Flagg, 1909-12). Charles Scribner, the son of the founder of the Scribner publishing company and, by 1879, the president of the firm, married the sister of architect Ernest Flagg. As a result, the Scribner family became one of Flagg's major patrons, commissioning their famous Fifth Avenue store and many other buildings. Fortunately for the Scribners, Flagg was one of the most talented architects of the era, interpreting contemporary French architectural principles in a manner far more sophisticated than that of his contemporaries. For his sister and brother-in-law, Flagg designed a beautifully integrated brick and marble townhouse with carefully arranged windows, simple classical moldings, and projecting balcony and cornice. The main entry is through an arch designed to allow automobile access; an elevator took the car to the basement. The facade was restored in 1994.

UES25 45 East 66th Street

Northeast corner Madison Avenue (Harde & Short, 1906-08). Harde & Short designed some of New York's finest early 20th-century apartment buildings, including the highly ornate Alwyn Court on Seventh Avenue and 58th Street of 1907-09 and this building with its lavish facades of red brick bound by black mortar and high-

Continue east to the corner of Madison Avenue.

45 East 66th Street in 1908

lighted with white terra-cotta detail. Harde & Short's fanciful adaptation of French Gothic design contrasts with the Italian Renaissance forms favored by most other apartment-house architects. The round corner tower, reminiscent of a medieval French château, anchors the building and draws attention to the boisterous ornament, the multi-paned windows, and the deep copper cornice. The earliest luxury apartment house on Madison Avenue, No. 45 originally had two apartments per floor, with bedrooms occupying the corner tower. There were no stores, but as Madison Avenue evolved, shops were inserted, including one that replaced the original corner entrance in 1929. By the 1970s, the owner of the building had allowed it to deteriorate to the point that the tenants went on a rent strike; residents also successfully petitioned for designation as an individual landmark. In 1987-89, as part of the conversion into a cooperative, a superb restoration revitalized the extraordinary facades.

UES26 Seventh Regiment Armory

643 Park Avenue between 66th and 67th streets (Charles W. Clinton, 1877-79). The Seventh Regiment's fortress-like armory is the single major survivor from the period before the New York Central's railroad tracks were roofed over and Park Avenue, south of 96th Street, developed into an exclusive residential boulevard. What was eventually to become the Seventh Regiment was organized in 1806 as a volunteer militia with members drawn from many of New York's most prominent families. After successful service in the Civil War, the Seventh Regiment campaigned for a new armory, finally persuading the city to lease, at no cost, the block between Park and Lexington avenues and 66th and 67th streets. Charles Clinton, a veteran of the Seventh, designed what is generally considered to be the prototypic model for the urban armory — a medieval-inspired administration building set in front of a large drill shed. The massive brick administration building, with its heavy base and mock-fortress features — such as crenellations and slits for crossbow arrows — is an imaginative structure borrowing elements from various medieval styles. The

Cross Madison Avenue and walk east on East 66th Street, past architect Mott B. Schmidt's Colonial Revival apartment house (1923-24) at No. 53, to Park Avenue.

arched drill hall is supported by iron trusses resembling those of contemporary railroad station sheds.

Urban armories not only served as drill halls for volunteer militia, but were also private men's clubs with appropriately elaborate interior decor. No regiment was more exclusive than the Seventh, known as the "silk stocking" regiment, and the interiors of its armory reflect that status. The armory contains some of the finest surviving 19th-century rooms in America, including the Veterans' Room and Library (now the Trophy Room), which were the earliest major commissions of the Associated Artists, the decorating firm established by Louis Comfort Tiffany. Other rooms were decorated by Alexander Roux & Co., L. Marcotte Co., Herter Brothers, and Pottier & Stymus, all leading American decorating firms. The armory was endangered in 1980-81 by an imprudent plan to construct a highrise luxury hotel or apartment building above the drill hall and, more recently, by proposals to mar the interiors with exposed sprinklers. A preservation campaign spearheaded by the Friends of the Armory was successful in gaining landmark designation for much of the interior in 1994.

Cross Park Avenue, turn left, and walk to 67th Street.

UES27 660 Park Avenue

Northwest corner East 67th Street (York & Sawyer, 1926-27). This strikingly austere Italian Renaissance-inspired building, clad entirely in limestone, is one of the most luxurious apartment houses on Park Avenue. When the thirteen-story cooperative was completed it had only eleven apartments, including an unprecedented 27-room triplex maisonette — a single unit that included the first three floors and had its own private entrance on 67th Street. It was specifically planned for Virginia Vanderbilt, but she never moved in (see CH18). The layout of this apartment can be gleaned from the arrangement of the windows. On the first and second floors were double-height public rooms, including a salon that was 46 feet long. The bedrooms were at the third floor; service facilities occupied all three floors on the west end of the apartment, overlooking 67th Street. Apparently, the apartment is still intact.

Continue north to 68th Street.

UES28 Harold I. and Harriet Barnes Pratt House

(Now Council on Foreign Relations), 58 East 68th Street,
southwest corner Park Avenue (Delano & Aldrich, 1919-
21). Unlike four of his older brothers who erected
houses opposite their childhood home on Clinton
Avenue in Brooklyn, Harold Pratt, one of the six sons of
Standard Oil vice-president and Pratt Institute founder
Charles Pratt, opted to build on fashionable Park Avenue.
Although Delano & Aldrich is most famous for its Neo-
classical houses of brick with stone trim, as represented
by the nearby Sloane House (UES29), the firm also produced several townhouses with finely detailed stone
fronts. As is typical of Delano & Aldrich's work, the Pratt
House has flat facades articulated by a deceptively simple
pattern of windows in varied shapes. Subtle ornamental
features, including a band of sea shells and the central
pediment on Park Avenue, serve as accents.

UES29 "Park Avenue Houses"

Park Avenue, west side between East 68th and 69th
streets: Percy and Maude Pyne House (now Americas
Society), 680 Park Avenue, (McKim, Mead & White,
1906-12); Oliver and Mary Pyne Filley House (now
Spanish Institute), 684 Park Avenue (McKim, Mead &
White, 1925-26); William and Frances Sloane House
(now Italian Cultural Institute), 686 Park Avenue
(Delano & Aldrich, 1916-19); Henry P. and Kate T. Davi-
son House (now Consulate General of Italy), 690 Park
Avenue (Walker & Gillette, 1916-17). Although used for
a wide variety of buildings, the Colonial Revival was
most popular for urban townhouses, as is evident on this
extraordinary block which is entirely lined with red
brick dwellings inspired by 18th-century architecture.
The earliest of the four is the corner house built by
financier Percy Pyne. This is a major work by McKim,
Mead & White, the firm responsible for New York's earliest Colonial Revival townhouses, erected during the
1890s. Charles McKim's design, a complex and dynamic
adaptation of the Colonial idiom, typifies the high quality of the firm's work.

   The three later houses, designed by a second genera-

*Pyne House in 1911
with rowhouses
(right) erected in
1881*

tion of Neo-classicists, are more chaste. This is not only
true at Delano & Aldrich's house at No. 686, designed for
a partner in the W.& J. Sloane furniture store, but also in
the Filley House at No. 684, designed by McKim, Mead
& White (following the death of the original partners)
for the Pynes' daughter and son-in-law. Walker &
Gillette's house on the corner of 69th Street, commissioned by one of the founders of Bankers Trust, is perhaps the most English of the four residences, resembling
the townhouses of Georgian London more than those of
Colonial America.

During the Christmas season of 1965, just as the City
Council was debating the establishment of the Land-
marks Commission, demolition began on the two
McKim, Mead & White houses and on the adjacent J.
William and Margaretta Clark House, at 49 East 68th
Street (Trowbridge & Livingston, 1913-14). Scaffolding
had been erected and interior features removed when the
Marquesa de Cuevas (born Margaret Rockefeller) stepped
in and anonymously purchased the properties. An edito-
rial in the *New York Times* proclaimed this the "Miracle on

68th Street," and went on to argue for the passage of the Landmarks law. The houses were designated as individual landmarks in 1970, eleven years before the designation of the Upper East Side Historic District.

UES30 Hunter College

695 Park Avenue between East 68th and 69th streets (Shreve, Lamb & Harmon, 1938-41). The Normal College for Women was organized by New York City in 1868, primarily as a teachers' training school, and was renamed in 1914 to honor its long-time president Thomas Hunter. After a fire destroyed the original Gothic Revival buildings in 1936, a replacement was commissioned that would meet the complex needs of what was still a women's college. Shreve, Lamb & Harmon's unadorned structure, one of the earliest Modern public buildings in New York, was controversial, prompting an *Architectural Forum* critic to write in 1940 that "the more sentimental section of the public and profession decry...the omission of the customary collegiate [i.e. Gothic] trimmings."

UES31 Union Club

701 Park Avenue, northeast corner East 69th Street (Delano & Aldrich, 1931-32). The Union is New York's oldest social club, founded in 1836 by men from the city's elite families. In 1927, the club's members voted to move from their Midtown home to the Upper East Side and this corner site was purchased. However, a lease on the property prevented demolition of an earlier mansion until 1932. Despite the Depression, the Union Club went ahead with Delano & Aldrich's $850,000 scheme. The dull, somewhat overblown exterior is designed in an English Renaissance manner that alludes to the gentlemen's clubs of London, but lacks the finesse of the clubs on Pall Mall.

UES32 The Asia Society

725 Park Avenue, northeast corner East 70th Street (Edward Larabee Barnes, 1979-81). Founded in 1956 by John D. Rockefeller 3rd, the Asia Society's first home was

Walk to the corner of East 69th Street.

Continue north to East 70th Street. Note the two early houses, survivors from a row of ten, at 709 and 711 Park Avenue (Bassett Jones, 1882-85).

*Sketch for the figures
at the fourth story of
the Lamont House*

an early International Style glass structure at 112 East
64th Street designed in 1958 by Philip Johnson. By
1979, the expanded collection had outgrown that building and this prominent new museum was erected. The
massing of architect Edward Larabee Barnes's red granite
building takes into consideration the wall of apartment
houses on Park Avenue and the more intimate rowhouses on East 70th Street.

Turn right on East
70th Street.

UES33 Thomas and Florence Lamont House
(Now Visiting Nurse Service of New York), 107 East
70th Street (Walker & Gillette, 1920-21). The Lamont
House, erected for a banker who became chairman of
J.P. Morgan & Co., is the most significant New York
example of a building designed in the "Jacobethan"
Revival style, a melange of English 16th- and early 17th-
century Elizabethan and Jacobean architectural forms.
Among the features of the style visible here are dark-col-
ored rough brick with light stone trim, large leaded-
glass windows separated by thick stone mullions, heavy
ornamental detail at the entrance and balustrade, and
whimsical carved figures on the beltcourse above the
fourth story. The pronounced gable ends and clustered
chimney stacks rising above the side garden lend this
urban dwelling the picturesque quality of an English
country house.

Continue east on
70th Street to No.
124. Note the va-
riety of house
fronts, most dating
from the early
20th century, with
their fine stone
and iron detail.

UES34 Edward A. Norman House
124 East 70th Street (William Lescaze, 1940-41). In

1940 financier Edward A. Norman purchased a house in the middle of this block and had William Lescaze redesign it in a deceptively simple Modern style that is in marked contrast to the more traditional facades on neighboring residences. The building is clad in glazed grayish brick chosen because it could be easily cleaned. Large rectangular window openings are filled with industrial metal sash and glass block. Lescaze created a series of ambiguous planar and textural relationships by contrasting the shiny brick, translucent glass blocks, and clear glass windows.

UES35 Stephen and Susan Clark House

Walk back to Park Avenue and continue west on East 70th Street.

(Now Explorers Club), 46 East 70th Street (Frederick Sterner, 1911-12). Like the nearby Lamont House (UES33), this is a romantic adaptation of the forms found on English country houses of the late 16th and early 17th centuries. This prototype is evident in the choice of materials and in the use of twin gables, octagonal turrets, a Tudor-arched entrance, and leaded-glass windows with stained-glass insets. Stephen Clark, heir to the Singer Sewing Machine fortune, was a well-known philanthropist and art collector (his collection was split between the Metropolitan Museum and Yale University), perhaps best known as the founder of the Baseball Hall of Fame in Cooperstown, N.Y.

UES36a Arthur S. and Adele Lewisohn Lehman House, 45 East 70th Street (Aymar Embury II, 1928-29), UES36b Walter and Florence Hope House, 43 East 70th Street (Mott B. Schmidt, 1928-29), and UES36c Walter and Carola Rothschild House, 41 East 70th Street (Aymar Embury II, 1928-29).

The block bounded by Madison and Park avenues and East 70th and 71st streets was among the last in the neighborhood to see residential development, as it was the location of Presbyterian Hospital from its incorporation in 1868 until its move to Washington Heights in 1928. With the demolition of the hospital, lots were sold, apartment houses erected on the avenues, and large townhouses built on the side streets. Although displaying different styles, these three houses illustrate the restrained quality of mainstream design at the end of the 1920s. No. 41 was commissioned by A&S chairman Walter Rothschild (he was the grandson of the store's founder Abraham Abraham); No. 43 was built by lawyer and Republican party leader Walter Hope; and No. 45 was the home of investment banker Arthur Lehman and his wife, philanthropist Adele Lehman, the donor of Lehman Hall to Barnard College. The Lehman House was purchased in 1966 by cosmetics manufacturers Joseph and Esteé Lauder.

UES37 Henry Clay and Adelaide Childs Frick House

(Now The Frick Collection), 1 East 70th Street (Carrère & Hastings, 1913-14). From 1877 until 1911 architect Richard Morris Hunt's famous Lenox Library stood on Fifth Avenue between 70th and 71st streets. In 1895 the library became a founding constituent of the New York Public Library and eleven years later the site was sold to industrialist Henry Clay Frick. Frick had to wait until 1911, when the collection moved to its new home on Fifth Avenue and 42nd Street, to begin demolition. Henry Clay Frick was a complex and multifaceted individual. His enormous fortune derived from coke and steel interests and from his service as a director of the Carnegie Steel Company. He was among the most truculent capitalists and virulently anti-union leaders of his day, perhaps best remembered as the instigator of the bloody Homestead Strike of 1892 at the Carnegie Steel plant in Homestead, Pennsylvania. On the other hand, Frick's artistic sensibility was extraordinarily sophisticated, and, with the assistance of art dealer Joseph Duveen, he assembled one of the world's premier art collections.

It was apparently Duveen who chose Thomas Hastings to design Frick's home and gallery (Hastings's partner John Carrère had died in 1911). From the start, Frick insisted on a building that could be converted into a museum, since he intended that his collection be opened to the public after he and his wife had died. On the Fifth

Continue west on the south side of 70th Street. Cross Madison Avenue and proceed down 70th Street to the Frick Collection on the corner of Fifth Avenue.

Avenue plot, Hastings was able to provide substantial
public and private rooms, New York's largest private art
gallery, and a generous garden, all in the manner of the
grand urban houses of 18th-century France. The three-
story, U-shaped building is faced entirely in limestone.
The Fifth Avenue front is enlivened by projecting central
bays with arched windows and Ionic pilasters and by a
colonnaded gallery wing which has pediments carved
by Attilio Piccirilli. Henry and Adelaide Frick moved
into the house in 1914 with their daughter and, according to a 1915 census tabulation, 27 servants. The servants were a multi-ethnic group haling from many parts
of Europe, and included one African-American — a 40
year-old employed as a "choreman" (live-in African-
American servants were very rare in New York's wealthiest households during this period). Following the death
of Mrs. Frick in 1931, architect John Russell Pope added
the entrance pavilion on 70th Street and made some

*Frick Residence in
1919*

changes for the conversion into a public museum. A museum expansion to the east entailed the demolition of two rowhouses visible in the accompanying photograph.

Walk north on Fifth Avenue to East 72nd Street.

907 Fifth Avenue in 1916

UES38 907 Fifth Avenue

Southeast corner East 72nd Street (J.E.R. Carpenter, 1915-16). The design of 907 Fifth, the third luxury apartment house on Fifth Avenue, is clearly modeled on the trend-setting Italian Renaissance palazzo form employed so successfully by McKim, Mead & White at 998 Fifth Avenue (MM13). This building had even more palatial interiors, with some apartments of over 25 rooms. It had the added advantage of being located on a prime corner site, with the windows of major rooms overlooking either Fifth Avenue and Central Park, or wide 72nd Street.

Turn right onto 72nd Street.

UES39a Oliver Gould and Mary Brewster Jennings House, 7 East 72nd Street (Flagg & Chambers, 1898-99) and UES39b Henry and Jessie Sloane House, (both now Lycée Français de New-York), 9 East 72nd Street (Carrère & Hastings, 1894-96). These limestone-clad buildings are two of the finest Beaux-Arts townhouses in New York. The dynamic sculptural quality of Beaux-Arts design, displayed in the exuberant detail and prominent mansard roofs, is especially evident at the Sloane House with its projecting Ionic columns, curvaceous stone balcony, and lush entrance cartouche. At the Jennings House, the visual play of recessed windows and projecting balconies with elaborate ironwork and the use of boldly tooled stonework creates an animated street front. Note, in particular, the fine vermiculation on the base; vermiculation is a classical conceit that imitates, in carved stone, the patterns that worms make in wood. The cartouche was the favorite ornamental device of Beaux-Arts designers since it could be molded into a variety of sculptural forms. There are 18 cartouches on the Jennings' facade — seven alone on the copper crest of the mansard!

Continue east on 72nd Street.

UES40 19 East 72nd Street
Northwest corner Madison Avenue (Rosario Candela; Mott B. Schmidt, consulting architect 1936-37). For the design of this subtly asymmetrical limestone high-rise, with its unusual streamlined base, the socially well-connected architect Mott B. Schmidt served as consultant to Rosario Candela, one of the leading apartment house designers of the inter-war period. The whimsical human and animal figures surrounding the entrance are the work of Carl P. Jennewein, a prominent traditional sculptor of the era.

UES41 Gertrude Rhinelander Waldo House
(Now Polo/Ralph Lauren Store), 867 Madison Avenue, southeast corner East 72nd Street (Kimball & Thompson,

1895-98). This extraordinary house was commissioned by Gertrude Rhinelander Waldo, although she never moved in; evidence suggests that she ran out of money before being able to complete the building. One of the largest private residences in New York City, it was designed to resemble such early 16th-century Loire Valley châteaux as Blois and Chambord. Mimicking its French prototypes, the Waldo house combines late Gothic and early Renaissance motifs, including statues of a monk, a knight, and other medieval personages ensconced in second-story niches, and a roofline that bristles with projecting dormers, finials, and chimneys. The house remained unoccupied until 1920 when it received its first commercial tenant. It was transformed into the flagship Polo/Ralph Lauren shop in the mid-1980s.

Turn left on Madison Avenue. Walk north to 73rd Street and turn left.

UES42 Joseph and Kate Pulitzer House

11 East 73rd Street (McKim, Mead & White, 1900-03). After his house on East 55th Street burned in 1900, Joseph Pulitzer had Stanford White design a new home

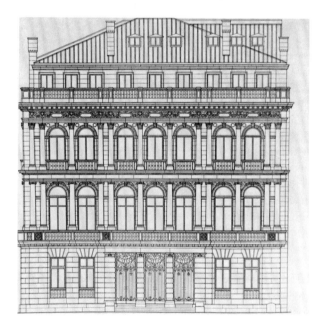

McKim, Mead & White drawing of the Pulitzer House

on this large mid-block site. White created one of New York's finest urban mansions, using forms borrowed from late 17th-century Venetian architecture. The horizontal composition, the solidity of the rusticated base, and the contrasting openness of the arcades of the upper stories reflect the influence of Baldassare Longhena's palaces on the Grand Canal. The building is unusual for a mid-block residence in that it has a small garden to the west; the garden front is a simplified version of the main elevation. In 1934 the house was converted into spacious apartments.

Joseph Pulitzer was one of America's legendary newspapermen. He was the publisher of the *New York World*, where he introduced an immensely popular and profitable policy of sensational reporting known as "yellow journalism." Pulitzer was a generous donor to philanthropic causes related to journalism, contributing the money that organized the Columbia University School of Journalism and establishing the Pulitzer Prize. He was also the donor of the Pulitzer Fountain in Grand Army Plaza (UES1). So sensitive was Pulitzer to noise, that he had a sound-proof wing, set on ball bearings, added to the rear of the house in 1904.

Return to Madison Avenue.

UES43 Madison Avenue Presbyterian Church

917 Madison Avenue, northeast corner East 73rd Street (James E. Ware & Sons, 1899-1901; parish house, James Gamble Rogers, 1916-17). What is now the Madison Avenue Presbyterian Church was organized in 1839 as the Eleventh Presbyterian Church. Considering its present fashionable location, it is ironic that the congregation was originally located on East 4th Street and Avenue D and ministered primarily to the workers in the nearby shipyards. The congregation moved north several times, finally settling on Madison Avenue and East 73rd Street in 1899 when it replaced an earlier church on the site with James E. Ware & Sons' simple Neo-Gothic structure. The Venetian Renaissance style parish house, located to the north, originally included such amenities as boys' and girls' gyms, a bowling alley, a swimming pool, and a roof garden that could be used for outdoor services.

Turn left on
Madison Avenue.
Walk to East 74th
Street and turn
right.

*Kramer House and
flanking rowhouses,
c.1935*

UES44 Raymond and Mildred Kramer House

32 East 74th Street (William Lescaze, 1934-35). In the
same year that he completed New York's first Modern
house (his own home and office at 211 East 48th Street),
architect William Lescaze was commissioned to design a
new townhouse for textile executive Raymond C.
Kramer and his wife Mildred; she was a personal friend
of the architect. Lescaze specialized in simple, carefully
balanced buildings that employ such industrial materials
as metal window sash and glass block in a straightfor-
ward manner. Here, the wall of glass block lights the
top-story living room. Lescaze favored this material
because it created private but well-illuminated interiors
that also allowed light to flow onto the street after dark.

Lescaze's modern aesthetic is in marked contrast to the design of the intact Italianate rowhouse to the left (D. & J. Jardine, 1870-71) and the rowhouse to the right that was altered by George A. Glanzer in a conservative Gothic manner in 1906.

UES45 Whitney Museum of American Art

945 Madison Avenue, southeast corner East 75th Street (Marcel Breuer & Associates, 1963-66). The building designed by Marcel Breuer for the Whitney Museum is one of the most important works of Modern architecture in New York City. Gertrude Vanderbilt Whitney founded the museum in 1930 after the Metropolitan Museum rejected the proposed donation of her collection of modern American art. The Whitney was initially located on West 8th Street, later moving to a site adjacent to the Museum of Modern Art. By 1961, the Whitney's directors realized that they needed a new building, both to house the growing collection and to establish a strong independent identity. Choosing this prominent site on Madison Avenue, they asked Bauhaus-trained modernist Marcel Breuer to design the structure. For his first museum, Breuer and his assistant Hamilton Smith created a building with a distinctive character that is instantly recognizable as the Whitney.

The Whitney is a functional building, with a glass enclosed entrance lobby inviting patrons into the building, and three full gallery floors that create an environment for viewing art that is not disturbed by outside influences. It is an expressive, sculptural work; the spare design emphasizing the properties of natural and man-made materials. This is evident on the exterior where granite, flame treated to heighten the natural grain, and cast concrete, seen on the end walls and quirky entrance canopy, are elegantly employed. The structurally daring cantilevered form, often referred to as a "reversed ziggurat," permitted Breuer to create ever-larger galleries on each successive floor; symbolically these "steps," with their curious skewed windows, create an inviting sense of mystery that beckons visitors to enter and explore the museum's interior.

As you return to Madison Avenue, note the handsome Colonial Revival house at No. 33 designed in 1901 by Grosvenor Atterbury. Cross Madison Avenue and turn right.

Turn left onto East 75th Street.

UES46 East 75th Street between Madison and Fifth Avenues.

Speculative residential development engulfed this street in the late 1870s and 1880s and a few of the houses erected during this period survive at the east end of the block. However, the predominant character on the street is that of early 20th-century residences erected for wealthy households. Among the grandest is the large French-inspired house at No. 3 designed in 1902 by C.P.H. Gilbert for Stuart Duncan. In the 1910 United States census, Duncan is listed as "mfr. worcestershire sauce." He was, in fact, the head of John Duncan & Son, a sauce manufacturer that became the now famous Lea & Perrins company. One of the most interesting features distinguishing this block is the abundance of ironwork, including not only the spectacular fence on the Fifth Avenue corner (UES47), but also Duncan's tall fence and iron-grille door; the balcony, door, and window guards at No. 4 (Trowbridge, Colt & Livingston, 1895-96), once the home of IBM founder Thomas J. Watson; and the cast-iron railings at Nos. 5 and 7 (Welsh, Smith & Provot, 1901-02).

Walk to the corner of Fifth Avenue.

UES47 Edward and Mary Harkness House

(Now Commonwealth Fund), 1 East 75th Street, North-east corner of Fifth Avenue (Hale & Rogers, 1907-09). Stephen Harkness, one of John D. Rockefeller's early Standard Oil partners, built this Italian Renaissance-inspired house as a wedding gift for his son and daughter-in-law. Although deceptively simple overall, this is a sophisticated work, with carefully placed ornamental highlights. Little expense was spared in creating a lavish house; it is clad in white marble and protected by an extraordinary fence that is a masterpiece of wrought-iron art. When the 1910 census enumerator came to the Harkness House, the family was not in residence; however, there were eight servants living here, all of whom were Swedish. This appears to reflect an ethnic bias on the part of New York's wealthiest residents who often sought out white Protestant servants, especially those from England, Scotland, and Scandinavia.

Although Edward Harkness was involved in railroad financing and served as a director of several railroad companies, his primary interest was the distribution of his vast inherited wealth; he inherited so much money that in 1926 he paid the sixth largest income tax in the country — $1,531,708! Harkness apparently established an excellent rapport with architect James Gamble Rogers during the design and construction of this house, since Rogers became the architect of many of the buildings financed by Harkness, including Butler Library at Columbia University, the original buildings of the Columbia-Presbyterian Medical Center, and the Harkness Memorial Quadrangle and Tower at Yale. In 1918, the house became the headquarters of the Commonwealth Fund, a foundation established by Edward Harkness' mother.

Harkness House, c. 1910

Tour II: The Metropolitan Museum of Art Historic District

Introduction

The Metropolitan Museum of Art Historic District is located in one of the most cosmopolitan sections of New York City, attracting residents and visitors from all over the world. The district, focussing on the great museum (an individual landmark, outside the district boundaries), was designated by the Landmarks Preservation Commission in 1977. It stretches along Fifth Avenue from 78th Street to 86th Street and incorporates many of the houses on the mid-blocks between Fifth and Madison avenues. The quality of architecture in the district is extraordinary, with what is unquestionably the finest block of turn-of-the-century townhouses in New York City (East 79th Street), the apartment building that was the prototype for many of the Upper East Side's luxury buildings (998 Fifth Avenue), and major works by some of America's most talented architects, including Carrère & Hastings, Ogden Codman, McKim, Mead & White, Horace Trumbauer, and Warren & Wetmore.

Begin: West Side of Fifth Avenue at 78th Street

Tour

MM1 Cook Block

The block bounded by Fifth and Madison avenues and East 78th and 79th streets was one of only two park blocks not developed during the initial period of building on the Upper East Side. The block was purchased by banker and railroad magnate Henry Cook in 1879. He built a house on the 78th Street corner (demolished), but held the remainder of the property for future development. In the late 1890s, Cook finally subdivided his property, selling lots to people of wealth and social stature who, between 1897 and 1912, erected the townhouses that still grace this extraordinary square block.

MM2a Payne and Helen Hay Whitney House

(Now Cultural Services, Embassy of France), 972 Fifth
Avenue and **MM2b Henry Cook House,** 973 Fifth
Avenue (both McKim, Mead & White, 1902-09). These
two granite houses, together with the flanking Duke
(MM3) and Fletcher (MM8) residences, form the only
remaining blockfront of individual townhouses on Fifth
Avenue, hinting at the grandeur of the avenue during
the brief period when it was almost entirely lined with
similarly imposing residences. Stanford White was
responsible for the design of this Italian Renaissance-
inspired double townhouse that appears, at first glance,
to be a single residence. The smaller house (No. 973), to
the north, was commissioned by Henry Cook, but he
died before it was completed. The house at No. 972 was
built as a wedding gift for Payne and Helen Whitney by
Whitney's uncle Oliver H. Payne. The beautifully proportioned bow-fronted residence, one of White's masterpieces, is ornamented with especially elegant carved
detail. Features of special note include the marble

Walk several
yards north on
Fifth Avenue to
the middle of the
block between
East 78th and
79th streets.

*Fifth Avenue, north
from 78th Street,
c. 1915 with the
Whitney and Duke
houses towards the
center*

*Whitney House
entrance hall, c. 1910*

entranceway, heavy wrought-iron doors, and the loggia
on the south elevation. The sumptuous interiors were
filled with antique columns, woodwork, and other
objects collected by White during his European travels.
The French government, which purchased the property
in 1952, sponsors public exhibitions in the house.

Return to 78th
Street and cross
to the southeast
corner of Fifth
Avenue and East
78th Street.

MM3 James B. and Nanaline Duke House

(now New York University Institute of Fine Arts), 1 East
78th Street, northeast corner Fifth Avenue (Horace
Trumbauer, 1909-12). This rare example of a freestand-
ing mansion in New York City bears a close resemblance
to the 18th-century Hôtel Labottière in Bordeaux. In a
manner typical of French Neo-classical architecture, the
Duke House has a projecting central entrance bay with
sculptural embellishment (notably in the pediment at
the roofline) flanked by more austere wings. Horace
Trumbauer ran the business side of his large Philadel-
phia-based office, leaving building design to others.
This house, like many of Trumbauer's projects, was
probably the work of his chief designer, Julian Francis
Abele, one of the first African-American architects in
America.

James B. Duke's rise from a poor North Carolina farm
boy to capitalist entrepreneur epitomizes the American

phenomenon of the self-made man. Duke's fortune was derived from tobacco; he was the founder and president of the American Tobacco Company and several related firms that together virtually monopolized the industry. Part of his fortune was used to found the North Carolina university that bears his family's name. The 1915 New York State Census records that Duke lived in this house with his wife and two-year-old daughter Doris, two relatives, and thirteen servants — three men and ten women — most of whom were immigrants from Scandinavia. Nanaline and Doris Duke gave the house to N.Y.U. in the late 1950s. The Institute has received an award from the New York Landmarks Conservancy for the superb adaptive reuse of the structure.

MM4 East 78th Street between Fifth and Madison Avenues

Continue east to the midblock of East 78th Street.

The two sides of this street provide a fascinating architectural contrast created by two different development patterns. In the 1870s and 1880s the south side was built up with speculative rowhouses. Remarkably, several of these survive, including the narrow Italianate brownstones at Nos. 22 and 26 (Silas M. Styles, architect/builder, 1871), the earliest intact houses in the historic district, and the Queen Anne house at No. 4 (Edward Kilpatrick, architect/builder, 1887-89). The construction of a new facade at No. 6 in 1913-14 (John Duncan, architect) instituted a wave of remodeling on the block, accounting for the irregular pattern of recessed and projecting fronts. In comparison, the north side consists of townhouses erected between 1897 and 1904 (No. 15 was redesigned in 1927), just after Henry Cook sold the lots. Despite the variety of styles, the north blockfront has a cohesive character created by a uniformity of scale and fairly consistent street wall.

MM5a Stuyvesant and Marian Fish House

Continue toward the corner of Madison Avenue.

25 East 78th Street, northwest corner Madison Avenue (McKim, Mead & White, 1897-1900) and **MM5b Philip and Beulah Rollins House,** 28 East 78th Street, southwest corner Madison Avenue (McKim, Mead & White,

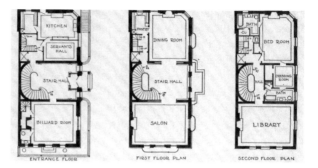

ENTRANCE FLOOR   FIRST FLOOR PLAN   SECOND FLOOR PLAN

1899-1902). These mansions are evidence that Madison Avenue was a prestigious location for grand residences at the turn of the century. The houses represent the two styles favored by the prestigious firm of McKim, Mead & White — the Italian Renaissance and the Colonial Revival. Stanford White's house for the Fishes is not one of his more successful Renaissance-inspired works. Despite some fine detail, especially the intertwining dolphins atop the fence posts, and the excellent restoration work undertaken in 1985, the yellow Roman brick facades appear to sag under the weight of the overscaled limestone trim.

In contrast, the Rollins house, with its variegated brickwork, delicate iron balconies, subtle limestone trim, and fluid interior plan is among McKim, Mead & White's finest essays in the Colonial Revival, beautifully combining features from a variety of 18th-century American and English sources. Philip Rollins, son of a western rancher and railroad developer, sold the family's ranches and, together with his wife, amassed a collection of over 300,000 items relating to the west which was donated to Princeton University in 1945. As he stated, the collection was assembled "to show that the West was not as wild as it was painted [by Hollywood]. Princeton is a great deal wilder."

Turn left on Madison Avenue, walk past several surviving townhouses and over a sidewalk designed in 1970 by Alexander Calder. Cross East 79th Street and look at the south side of the street.

MM6 East 79th Street, South Side, between Fifth and Madison Avenues

With almost every detail intact, the south side of the street is the finest surviving blockfront of turn-of-the-

century townhouses in New York. The character of
blocks such as this was succinctly described by Edith
Wharton in her novel, *The House of Mirth*, when she wrote
of the "new brick and limestone house fronts fantastically varied in obedience to the American craving for
novelty." A glance along the block shows the brick and
limestone (and two granite) houses to be "fantastically
varied," with facades based on American Colonial (Nos.
12 and 14; Little & Brown, 1901-03), English Georgian
(No. 16; Warren & Wetmore, 1901-03), French Neo-
classical (No. 18; see MM7), and other architectural
precedents. This seemingly incongruous juxtaposition
of architectural forms, so unlike what would be seen in a
European city, was castigated by some critics. However,
to the elite of American society, such novel eclecticism
and display of individuality were not seen as being the
least bit unseemly.

MM7 J. Woodward and Henriette Haven House
(Now Acquavella Gallery), 18 East 79th Street (Ogden
Codman, 1908-09). Francophile architect Ogden Codman (see CH22) was responsible for this sophisticated
design which adapts the form of 18th-century Neo-classical townhouses in Bordeaux to conditions in early
20th-century New York. On a lot only 30 feet wide,
Codman created a complex and refined work. The facade
is arranged with a subtle vertical emphasis; note how
beautifully the projecting arched pediment of the central
second-story window is balanced by the flanking third-
story balustrade railings.

MM8 Isaac and Mary Fletcher House
(Now Ukrainian Institute of America), 2 East 79th
Street, southeast corner Fifth Avenue (C.P.H. Gilbert,
1897-99). Although a house modeled after the châteaux
of France's Loire Valley might seem out of place in Manhattan, this was one of several mansions designed in this
mode. The Fletcher House is the finest of the three
château-like residences on Fifth Avenue designed by
C.P.H. Gilbert, a master of what is called the François I
style (see 990 Fifth Avenue, MM10; and Warburg

Walk west along
the north side
of 79th Street
towards Fifth
Avenue.

House, CH27). Here, the rural château form is compacted by the demands of an urban site, yet the house has a lively asymmetrical shape, and is complete with a moat-like areaway with front stairs suggestive of a draw bridge. The carved detail is outstanding: the winged monster ensconced on the chimney, the paired dolphins on the stone entrance railings, the rustic couples who flank the entrance, and the heads dripping from the second-floor window are but a few of the whimsical ornamental touches.

After the death of businessman Isaac Fletcher in 1917, the house was purchased by oil baron Harry Sinclair. Later it was home to Augustus van Horn Stuyvesant and his sister Ann Stuyvesant, the last direct descendants of Dutch Governor Peter Stuyvesant. The house has been the headquarters of the Ukrainian Institute since 1955 and is often open for public events.

Turn right onto Fifth Avenue.

MM9 980 and 985 Fifth Avenue

Northeast corner East 79th Street (Paul Resnick and Harry F. Green, 1965-68, and Wechsler & Schimenti, 1969-70). These two apartment buildings are not only excruciatingly banal works of architecture, but they rudely break the plane of the Fifth Avenue street wall. They replaced six townhouses, including four erected for clothier Isaac Brokaw and his children that were demolished, despite pleas for their preservation, in February, 1965 (see page 16). The ensuing *New York Times* editorial, entitled "Rape of the Brokaw Mansion," decried the "weekend stealth...[of] the despoilers" who demolished these buildings and noted that if the city did not pass pending landmarks legislation there would be no landmarks left to save. This outcry influenced Mayor Robert Wagner's decision, two months later, to sign the law creating the New York City Landmarks Preservation Commission.

Walk to the corner of Fifth Avenue and East 80th Street.

MM10 990 Fifth Avenue

Northeast corner East 80th Street (Rosario Candela, 1926-27). A glance up or down Fifth Avenue reveals that the apartment houses erected during the second and third decades of the 20th century are all approximately the same height and most share a common Italian Renaissance-inspired design. However, the width of each building's street frontage varies. Since these apartment houses replaced single-family dwellings (in this case, the François I style château designed in 1899 by C.P.H. Gilbert for dime-store magnate F.W. Woolworth), their size depends on the number of older residences a developer could amass. Although 990 Fifth Avenue is a relatively narrow structure (the lot is only 27'2" wide), the apartments were quite spacious — there were originally only six duplex cooperative units in the building.

Turn right onto East 80th Street.

F. W. Woolworth's French-inspired chateau, c. 1901

MM11 2, 4, and 6 East 80th Street

(C.P.H. Gilbert, 1911-16). F.W. Woolworth had his architect build these houses for his three daughters and their husbands. No. 2 was the home of Edna and

Return to Fifth Avenue and turn right. Note: The best views of buildings on Fifth Avenue can be obtained by walking on the west side of the street.

Franklyn Hutton and the birthplace of socialite Barbara Hutton (Hutton was married seven times — to three princes, a count, a baron, an international playboy, and movie star Cary Grant — and was often called "the poor little rich girl"). The central house, designed in the François I style that Gilbert loved, is flanked by nearly identical townhouses designed in an 18th-century French Neo-classical manner.

MM12 991 Fifth Avenue

(Now The American Irish Historical Society; Turner & Killian, 1900-01). This is one of several Fifth Avenue townhouses on the tour that were erected as speculative projects and not for individual clients. The house, with its combination of popular Colonial Revival and Beaux-Arts elements, illustrates the high quality of speculative real estate development at the turn of the century. The building was restored in 1991.

Continue north to East 81st Street.

MM13 998 Fifth Avenue

Northeast corner East 81st Street (McKim, Mead & White, 1910-12). 998 Fifth Avenue, the first luxury apartment building constructed on Fifth Avenue north of 59th Street, became the model for most of the apartment houses erected on the Upper East Side before the Great Depression. William Richardson, a partner in the firm of McKim, Mead & White, adapted the Italian Renaissance palazzo form that the firm had pioneered at such buildings as the Metropolitan Club (UES3). The tripartite horizontal massing typical of Italian Renaissance palaces has been expanded vertically to provide a twelve-story structure. The street elevations are faced with exquisitely carved limestone highlighted by panels of yellow Sienna marble at the eighth and twelfth stories, an unusual iron entrance canopy, and an especially striking cornice.

The building has always been referred to simply as "998," since, as the New York Times noted in 1913, "it is so famous that even the name of the Avenue is not added." The apartments were expansive in plan and sumptuous in appointment, consisting of both simplex units (with all rooms on one floor) and smaller duplexes (public

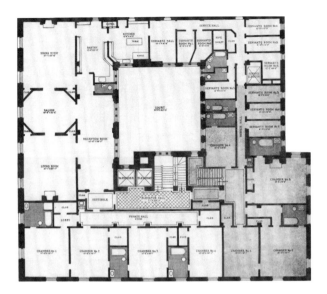

Plan of 998 Fifth Avenue

rooms on one floor and bedrooms above). The simplexes, overlooking Fifth Avenue, contained suites of public rooms that could be joined to create grand entertaining spaces over 35 feet wide and 70 feet long.

998 Fifth Avenue,
Elizabethan style reception room, 1912

At the time 998 was built, apartment house living had not yet been widely accepted by the very wealthy, but, as the *Real Estate Record* noted, 998 helped to change the "deep-seated repugnance" that "families of high social position" had for apartments. In order to attract residents, the rental agent (Douglas Elliman) instituted a novel marketing ploy. He rented the tenth floor, at a bargain price, to famous jurist and former Secretary of State Elihu Root, realizing that Root's presence would induce other socially prominent individuals to rent apartments. Each apartment contained a fairly extensive area for servants, with up to five small bedrooms (averaging about 6' x 12'); in 1915 the Root household consisted of not only Mr. and Mrs. Root and their son, but five servants — nurse, cook, waitress, parlor maid, and chamber maid. Curiously, during a period of widespread discrimination in housing, at least one apartment at 998 was rented to a member of the city's German-Jewish elite — financier and philanthropist Murray Guggenheim and his wife, Leonie.

Turn right onto East 81st Street and walk halfway down the block.

MM14 Grenville Lindall Winthrop House

15 East 81st Street (Julius F. Gayler, 1919-21). The Winthrop House is one of the most splendid Colonial Revival dwellings in New York City. The style was appropriate for Winthrop who traced his ancestry back to John Winthrop, the first governor of the Massachusetts Bay Colony. The long, elegantly proportioned street front of the slightly recessed red brick and white marble townhouse has an understated elegance that exemplifies the finest Colonial Revival design. A comparison of this house with its neighbor to the west (No. 11), designed by Julius Gayler five years after the Winthrop House, demonstrates why windows are such an important design feature of historic buildings. At the Winthrop House, the multi-paned window sash adds to the complex texture of the facade; whereas, at No. 11, the heavy plate-glass windows which replaced the original multi-paned sash (prior to the designation of the historic district) appear as holes in the facade, destroying the architect's original concept.

Return to Fifth Avenue. Turn right and walk to 82nd Street.

MM15 Metropolitan Museum of Art

1000 Fifth Avenue. The Metropolitan Museum of Art,
one of the world's preeminent art institutions, was
incorporated in 1870 and two years later was presented
by the city with a site in Central Park at 82nd Street. The
initial museum building, designed by Calvert Vaux and
Jacob Wrey Mould in 1874, was a picturesque Victorian
Gothic structure set into the park landscape (a wall of this
building survives within the present Lehman Wing). In
1894, as the surrounding area was beginning its transformation into an elite neighborhood, a substantial addition along Fifth Avenue was commissioned from Richard
Morris Hunt, one of America's foremost architects. The
addition changed the orientation of the museum from
the park to the city. The wing was the manifestation of
the belief of the Metropolitan's patrons that an impressive art museum was a necessity for a city that aspired to

Metropolitan Museum
of Art, c. 1903

international stature. The monumental classically-inspired design, with its arched entrances and projecting paired columns, reflects the influence of the grand pavilions at the World's Columbian Exposition held in Chicago in 1893, a year before the Metropolitan began its expansion. The exposition buildings (one designed by Hunt) were perceived as an expression of the triumph of American culture. The symbolic value of this monumental architectural statement was reasserted by Hunt for his work at the Metropolitan Museum. Subsequent wings along the avenue were designed by McKim, Mead & White (1904-26). More recent additions, part of a major expansion undertaken between 1971 and 1990, are the work of Kevin Roche, John Dinkeloo & Associates. Compare the relatively modest original staircase, visible in the accompanying photograph, with the expansive entrance stair built in the 1970s.

Cross Fifth Avenue (at this location, often referred to as "Museum Mile") to the Metropolitan's staircase.

MM16 1001 Fifth Avenue

(Johnson/Burgee, 1978-80). This controversial apartment house marks Philip Johnson and John Burgee's earliest foray into Post-Modern design. For the street facade (another architect did the rest of the building), Johnson/Burgee borrowed design elements, such as the rusticated limestone and the molding profiles, from the neighboring historic buildings. Note how the overscaled moldings do not extend to the ends of the new building. This is a playful visual device used by the architects to show that they are simply decorative and are not part of the building's structure. The mansard roof at 1009 Fifth Avenue (MM17) is echoed atop No.1001 by a false mansard-like front that hides the building's water tower.

Cross back to the east side of Fifth Avenue and walk to the northeast corner of Fifth Avenue and East 82nd Street.

MM17 1009 Fifth Avenue

Southeast corner East 82nd Street (Welch, Smith & Provot, 1899-1901). Among the firms most active in the construction of speculative townhouses on the Upper East Side was W.W. & T.M. Hall, who, along with architect Alexander M. Welch, were responsible for this impressive residence. The red Roman brick house features the profusion of sculptural detail, notably car-

1009 Fifth *Avenue*,
c. 1901

touches, that is characteristic of the Beaux-Arts style.
There is also fine ironwork at the window railings,
entrance canopy, and projecting breakfast nook, and an
impressive mansard roof capped by finials that were
replaced during an award-winning restoration completed in 1985.

MM18 East 82nd Street between Fifth and Madison Avenues

Walk partway
down East 82nd
Street.

The harmonious appearance of this block of East 82nd
Street results from a restrictive covenant, signed by

property owners in 1888-89 and expanded in 1900, that controlled how the lots were developed. The owners agreed to construct only "first class dwellings" of brick or stone, with facades set back five feet from the building line. All of the houses were erected on speculation between 1888 and 1901 and subsequently sold. Although no single house is of great individual interest, and many of the early facades on the south side were later altered, this remains one of the finest blocks in the historic district.

Return to Fifth Avenue and turn right.

MM19a 1016 Fifth Avenue

southeast corner East 83rd Street (John B. Peterkin, 1926-27) and **MM19b 1020 Fifth Avenue,** northeast corner East 83rd Street (Warren & Wetmore, 1924-25). Both of these apartment houses have Italian Renaissance-inspired facades clearly influenced by 998 Fifth Avenue (MM13). Although relatively tall buildings, they acknowledge the historic low-rise character of Fifth Avenue's residences. Each has a limestone base designed to relate to the scale of the earlier townhouses and to keep the eyes of the passerby focused at street level. This is accomplished at No. 1016 by three-story Corinthian pilasters and at No. 1020 by a two-story arcade.

Continue north toward East 84th Street. At No. 1025, note the length to which a developer will go for a Fifth Avenue address; this is the entrance to a 1955 apartment house located on 83rd and 84th streets!

MM20a 1026 and 1027 Fifth Avenue

Van Vleck & Goldsmith, 1901-03) and **MM20b Jonathan and Harriet Thorne House,** 1028 Fifth Avenue, southeast corner East 84th Street (C.P.H. Gilbert, 1901-03). All three of these houses, two of which are owned by the Marymount School, were erected at the same time, although each is an individual design in a sumptuous Beaux-Arts mode. The corner house was commissioned by leather manufacturer Jonathan Thorne and was his retirement home for the final 20 years of his life. The two midblock townhouses were erected as a speculative venture by marble dealer Benjamin A. Williams (No. 1027 is faced with marble). All three are crowned by mansard roofs and embellished with detail typical of Beaux-Arts design.

MM21 3 East 84th Street

(Howells & Hood, 1927-28). Joseph M. Patterson, the owner of the *Daily News*, commissioned this exceptionally urbane apartment house from Raymond Hood and his partner John Mead Howells

Turn right on East 84th Street.

3 East 84th Street in 1929

two years after the completion of the architects' Chicago Tribune Building (erected for a cousin of Patterson's), and two years before Hood designed the East 42nd Street headquarters for the New York newspaper. The Art Deco building was, according to a writer in *The New Yorker*, a translation of "many of the best features of new Paris apartments into an American vision." It was planned with a pied-à-terre on the top floors for Patterson's own use and a single apartment on each floor below. The asymmetrical design has a strong vertical emphasis that is in marked contrast to the horizontal expression found on the Italian Renaissance-inspired apartment houses that predominate in the district. The limestone facade features such classic Art Deco motifs as a band of zig-zag ornament, panels and railings with triangles and diamonds, and stylized foliage (notably on the front doors). The metal window spandrels, soon to become common on Art Deco buildings, are thought to have been introduced on this building.

MM22 William Starr and Edith Warren Miller House

1048 Fifth Avenue, southeast corner East 86th Street (Carrère & Hastings, 1912-14). This massive red brick and limestone corner mansion was modeled after early

Return to Fifth Avenue and turn right. Walk to 86th Street.

17th-century French buildings erected during the reign of Louis XIII, such as those in the Place des Vosges in Paris. This rather austere Renaissance style was a favorite of Carrère & Hastings, employed, for example, at their Staten Island Borough Hall. At the time of his death in 1935, the original owner of the house, businessman William Starr Miller, was described by the *New York Times* as "a retired capitalist." The mansion was later home to Mrs. Cornelius Vanderbilt and for many years was occupied by the YIVO Institute for Jewish Research. Plans call for its conversion into a museum.

Tour III: The Carnegie Hill Historic District

Introduction

The appellation, "Carnegie Hill," used to describe the neighborhood stretching from East 86th Street to East 96th Street, from Fifth Avenue to Lexington Avenue, dates from the first years of the 20th century, after Andrew Carnegie erected his mansion on Fifth Avenue and 91st Street. Carnegie purchased land in what was then referred to as "Prospect Hill," a section already well developed with rowhouses and a few modest apartment buildings and tenements. The decision by a man as wealthy as Carnegie to build on 91st Street had a tremendous affect on the character of the area; other mansions and a succession of luxury apartment buildings soon appeared throughout the neighborhood.

Carnegie Hill is the most varied section of the Upper East Side, with a complex development history that has created a fascinating variety of buildings. Here, virtually side-by-side, can be found modest rowhouses and enormous mansions, working-class tenements and luxury apartment houses, and the commercial and institutional buildings erected to serve the needs of a diverse population. Carnegie Hill is an exciting place to visit, for not only does it provide an array of fine architecture, but it contains five of the city's leading museums and, on Madison Avenue, a selection of fine restaurants, cafes, boutiques, and galleries.

The initial Carnegie Hill Historic District, designated in 1974, was a small area consisting of two non-contiguous units — one between Fifth and Madison avenues and the other between Madison and Park avenues. The district boundaries were substantially expanded in 1993.

Begin: East 86th
Street, just east of
Fifth Avenue

Tour

CH1   William and Elsie Woodward House

(Now Town Club), 9 East 86th Street (Delano & Aldrich, 1916-18). Delano & Aldrich, best known for its refined red brick Colonial Revival work, designed this restrained Neo-classical townhouse for the family of William Woodward. Woodward, president of the Hanover Bank, was probably best known during his life as a "turf leader"; two of his thoroughbreds won the Triple Crown (Omaha and Gallant Fox). Faced with gray Indiana limestone and trimmed in contrasting white Hautville marble, the house is notable for the austerity of its street frontage and for the placement of the entrance in a pavilion to the side of the main structure. The building was converted into a private club in 1957.

Walk to Fifth
Avenue and turn
right. Walk to East
87th Street and
turn right.

Woodward House,
c. 1918

CH2 Henry and Annie Phipps House

(Now Liederkranz Society), 6 East 87th Street
(Grosvenor Atterbury, 1902-04). The Italian Renaissance-inspired Phipps House, built for a partner in
Andrew Carnegie's steel empire, has a rather staid limestone facade enriched with exuberant ironwork at the
ground floor, a heavy carved balcony on the second
story, and double arched windows on the top. It typifies
Grosvenor Atterbury's designs for wealthy clients. Such
traditionally-styled townhouses helped subsidize Atterbury's more innovative work, notably his experiments
with affordable model housing. Atterbury designed several model tenements, was the architect of Forest Hills
Gardens in Queens, and invented a system for the mass
production of low-cost housing. The Liederkranz Society, a German singing organization, purchased the
house in 1949.

CH3 The Capitol

12 East 87th Street (George
& Edward Blum, 1910-11).
George & Edward Blum was
among the most creative
firms specializing in apartment house design in the
early years of the 20th century. The firm's best buildings, of which the Capitol is
an early example, are
embellished with an idio-
syncratic ornamental vocabulary. Here, the Blums
combined such traditional
forms as egg-and-dart

*George & Edward
Blum's drawing of
the Capitol*

moldings with more original geometric and organic features, to create a densely textured facade. The eight-
story building, originally containing only eight
apartments, is clad in white brick and glazed white terra
cotta with an "egg-shell" finish. The brackets at the
roofline once supported an impressive cornice, visible in
the Blums' drawing.

Return to Fifth
Avenue and turn
right.

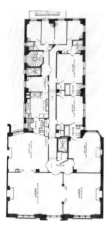

Plan of 1067 Fifth Avenue

CH4 1067 Fifth Avenue

(C.P.H. Gilbert, 1914-17). When the prolific townhouse architect C.P.H. Gilbert received the commission for Fifth Avenue's second luxury apartment house, he simply adapted the château-like features of his favorite François I style, seen at the Fletcher (MM8), Woolworth (MM10) and Warburg (CH27) houses, to the form of a tall building. The lively rooftop silhouette with dormers, the balcony railing ornamented with dolphins, and the fire-breathing dragons above the entrance are typical of the ornamental vocabulary that appears on Gilbert's better-known work in this style. Although constructed on a relatively narrow 50 x 100 foot lot, the building had spacious apartments that attracted such early residents as the families of Philip Armour (of the meat-packing dynasty), publisher and editor Robert Collier, politician W. Averell Harriman, and John Wanamaker (grandson of the founder of the eponymous department store).

CH5 Solomon R. Guggenheim Museum

1071 Fifth Avenue (Frank Lloyd Wright, design 1943-55; construction 1956-59). The dynamism of the Guggenheim, one of the masterpieces of 20th-century architecture, can best be appreciated from the southwest corner of Fifth Avenue and 88th Street where the view of the flowing rotunda is not marred by the static addition to the north, completed in 1992. The Guggenheim was organized as the Museum of Non-Objective Art with the purpose of displaying Solomon Guggenheim's collection of European abstract artwork. Guggenheim, prompted by his artistic advisor Hilla Rebay, commissioned Wright to design a suitable home for the collection. Wright's initial designs date from 1943-45, but he redesigned the museum several times as the site grew and as the trustees changed the nature of the institution following Guggenheim's death in 1949 and Rebay's subsequent ouster as museum director. Wright's organic structure is a complex interweaving of geometries, notably a small rotunda balanced by a large spiraling quarter-mile long exhibition space. The geometric forms were continued into the smallest details — even the sidewalks contain inset metal circles. One of Wright's greatest challenges (and one that can easily be understood by most New Yorkers) was persuading the conservative bureaucracy of the city's Department of Buildings to issue a permit for this novel structure. The building is constructed of concrete supported by a steel frame, with the exterior covered in Gunite, a mixture of cement and sand that was sprayed onto the structure and then painted white. The recent building project (Gwathmey Siegel & Associates, architect), included not only the unfortunate addition which disrupts the dynamic flow of Wright's rotunda, but also a fine restoration of the deteriorated exterior of the museum and beautifully executed work on the interior.

Turn right onto
East 88th Street.

*Entrance to 4 East
88th Street, c. 1925*

CH6 4 East 88th Street
(Electus D. Litchfield & Rogers, 1921-22). The massing,

proportions, and subtle detail here create what is perhaps New York City's finest Colonial-inspired apartment house. The building is faced with red brick laid in traditional Flemish bond and retains its original multi-paned window sash. Imagine how the design would suffer if these exquisite windows, with their pattern of raised wooden mullions, were replaced by the blank single-pane windows that have appeared on so many other apartment houses in the neighborhood. The facade contains one especially wonderful detail — the small carved heads that rise from the arched entrance pediment; one of these is clearly George Washington, peering off into Central Park.

CH7a 5, 7, and 9 East 88th Street

(Turner & Killian, 1901-03), and **CH7b Fulton and Mary Cutting House,** 15 East 88th Street (Delano & Aldrich, 1919-22). The three Beaux-Arts style brick and limestone houses designed by Turner & Killian were erected as speculative ventures, while the Cutting House was one of four Colonial Revival townhouses commissioned by banker R. Fulton Cutting for his children (see CH9). Fulton Cutting was a pioneer in the development of the radio, producing the first mass-produced bedside model, sold at a cost of $10.00 each.

Walk to Madison Avenue and turn left. Proceed to 89th Street and turn left.

CH8 Graham House

22 East 89th Street, southwest corner Madison Avenue (Thomas Graham, 1891-93). This exuberant Romanesque Revival building was commissioned by and named for Thomas Graham, one of the most active builders in Carnegie Hill. Graham House was planned as an apartment hotel, a building type that was becoming increasingly popular in the 1890s. As was typical of apartment hotels, this structure had suites without kitchens; residents generally took their meals in the hotel's first-floor dining room. The rather simple seven-story facade is clad in gold Roman brick trimmed with limestone detail (note the two stone plaques on the second floor with their Byzantine carving and grimacing faces). The outstanding feature is unquestionably the entrance with its

complex buttressed arch, stout twisted columns, rich foliate carving, and pair of carved winged monsters.

Drawing of Graham House, 1891

CH9 Cutting Houses

(Now St. David's School), 12, 14, and 16 East 89th Street (Delano & Aldrich, 1919-22). In 1919, R. Fulton Cutting, a prominent financier, political reformer, and philanthropist, commissioned houses for four of his children — three on 89th Street and one on 88th Street (CH7b). These are among Delano & Aldrich's most refined Colonial Revival works. They exemplify *Architectural Record's* 1923 description of the firm's style: "there is a small amount of ornament, very telling because well placed and brought into strong accent by contrast with simple planes and wide wall spaces." On the Cutting Houses, the planar brick facades are linked by a continuous ground-floor arcade, an iron balcony, a limestone cornice, and a two-story mansard roof, all contributing to the illusion of a single large mansion.

Continue west on 89th Street, passing the National Academy of Design's school at No. 5, and the brick 89th Street wing of the Huntington House (CH10) at No. 3. Turn right onto Fifth Avenue.

83

CH10 Archer and Helen Huntington House

(Now National Academy of Design), 1083 Fifth Avenue
(Ogden Codman, 1913-15). In 1902 Archer Huntington, the stepson of California railroad magnate Collis P.
Huntington, purchased one of three newly-built Beaux-
Arts townhouses on Fifth Avenue between 89th and 90th
streets. Eleven years later he had architect Ogden Codman remove the brick and limestone front and replace it
with a more sedate French Neo-classical facade of limestone. In addition, Codman redesigned the interiors and
added the 89th Street wing. The choice of the Francophile Codman is somewhat curious since Huntington's life was dedicated to the study of Spanish civilization — he was the founder of the Hispanic Society
of America and built the Audubon Terrace museum
complex on Broadway and 155th Street that includes that
institution. In 1940 Huntington and his second wife, the
sculptor Anna Hyatt Huntington, donated the house and
the lot at 5 East 89th Street to the National Academy of
Design which erected a school (William Platt, 1957-59)
and opened the structure to the public as a museum.

CH11 Church of the Heavenly Rest

1084-87 Fifth Avenue, southeast corner East 90th Street
(Mayers, Murray & Phillip, 1926-29). The Episcopal
congregation of the Church of the Heavenly Rest,
founded in 1865, was housed in a rather dilapidated
building on Fifth Avenue and 45th Street when, in 1924,
it was offered this property on Fifth Avenue and 90th
Street by Mrs. Andrew Carnegie; her offer stipulated that
plans for a new building receive her approval. Andrew
Carnegie had acquired this property in 1917 to ensure
that his house and garden (CH12) would not be placed
in shadow by the construction of a high-rise apartment
house. For its new building, the congregation commissioned a design from Mayers, Murray & Phillip, the successor firm of Bertram Goodhue (d. 1924). Following in
the tradition established by Goodhue at such masterpieces as St. Thomas Episcopal Church on Fifth Avenue
and St. Vincent Ferrer R.C. Church on Lexington Avenue,
Goodhue's successors designed the new church in the

"American Gothic" manner. The boldly massed structure was erected with a modern steel frame and has austere limestone facades articulated by large pointed-
arched openings and sculpted figures that seem to grow
organically from the stonework. This is especially evident at the entrance with its figures of Moses and John
the Baptist and its pair of winged angels. The front doors
are worth close examination; the metal hinges are
embossed with scenes of the history of religion (and this
church congregation) in New York City. The magnificent open plan interior features vibrantly-colored
abstract stained glass, fine carved woodwork, and a pul-
pit by sculptor Malvina Hoffman.

*Presentation drawing
for Church of the
Heavenly Rest,
c.1926*

CH12 Andrew and Louise Carnegie House

(Now Cooper-Hewitt, National Design Museum, Smithsonian Institution), 2 East 91st Street, southeast corner
Fifth Avenue (Babb, Cook & Willard, 1899-1902).
Shortly after Andrew Carnegie purchased this property
in 1898 he is quoted as having uttered the somewhat
curious statement concerning his plan to build "the
most modest, plainest and most roomy house in New

Continue north,
past Andrew
Carnegie's
garden (note the
original fence and
massive granite
sidewalk blocks),
to East 91st Street.
Turn right.

Garden and rear elevation of the Carnegie mansion with Kahn House, (CH13) and 1107 Fifth Avenue (CH28) to rear, c. 1925

York." At 64 rooms, the house was certainly roomy, befitting one of America's wealthiest men. Carnegie had made his fortune in steel, retiring in 1901 with a net worth of approximately $300 million. The Fifth Avenue house was planned as Carnegie's retirement home. Here he could amuse himself in his large garden, laid out by Schermerhorn & Foulks (the plan is largely intact and includes, at the east end, what the original plans refer to as a "rockery") and could meet with those involved in his favorite charitable endeavors, such as the construction of library buildings — he donated $5,000,000 for 66 branches of the New York Public Library. Carnegie desired a substantial house, but he was not an ostentatious social arbiter and did not want a pretentious structure. This residence combines the "homey" forms of the Colonial Revival, evident in the Flemish bond brickwork, with the fashionable robust ornament of Beaux-Arts design. It was the use of simple brickwork, on an avenue lined with grand marble and limestone palaces, that lends this large dwelling its "modest" and "plain" appearance.

In 1905, the New York State census records that this was home to Carnegie, his wife, and their daughter, as well as a German-born caretaker and his wife, and fourteen additional servants, all of whom were recent immigrants from Carnegie's native Scotland. Following Louise

Carnegie's death in 1946, the house was used by the Columbia University School of Social Work and in 1968 became the Cooper-Hewitt Museum. The Cooper-Hewitt's extensive collection of objects relating to all aspects of design was established at the Cooper Union in 1897 by Sarah and Eleanor Hewitt and closed in 1963, only to be saved by the Smithsonian Institution which accepted the donation of the collection and established the museum in 1968. The Carnegie Corporation donated the house to the Smithsonian and architect Hugh Hardy designed the sensitive museum conversion completed in 1976.

CH13 Otto and Addie Kahn House

(Now Convent of the Sacred Heart School), 1 East 91st Street, northeast corner Fifth Avenue (J. Armstrong Stenhouse and C.P.H. Gilbert, 1913-18). For this, one of the last New York mansions modeled after an Italian Renaissance palazzo, British architect J. Armstrong Stenhouse, in association with local practitioner C.P.H. Gilbert, chose as a model the Cancelleria in Rome. This 15th-century palazzo had also served as inspiration for McKim, Mead & White's Villard Houses on Madison Avenue and 50th Street, the buildings that introduced the Renaissance palazzo form to New York residential architecture over 30 years earlier. At the Kahn house, the architects adapted features of the Roman palace in a somewhat literal manner, using them in the creation of an individual work appropriate for the lifestyle of a wealthy early 20th-century New York family. Especially novel features are the enclosed drive which allowed family and guests to arrive in their new automobiles without public scrutiny and the impressive interior courtyard.

The enormous house was commissioned by Otto Kahn, a partner in the banking firm of Kuhn, Loeb & Co. During their lives, Mr. and Mrs. Kahn were best known as lavish patrons of the arts; the Metropolitan Opera was a favored recipient of their largesse. As at the Carnegie House across the street, the Kahns had a large staff. In 1925, Mr. and Mrs. Kahn and their two children were

The interior courtyard of the Kahn House in 1919

served by fourteen live-in employees, but unlike Carnegie's staff, the Kahn's servants were a multinational group, including people from Scotland, England, Ireland, Norway, and Switzerland. Shortly after her husband's death in 1934, Addie Kahn sold the house to the Convent of the Scared Heart which uses the building as a school for girls. The building was cleaned and restored in 1994.

CH14a James A. and Florence Sloane Burden House

(Now Convent of the Sacred Heart), 7 East 91st Street (Warren, Wetmore & Morgan, 1902-05) and **CH14b John Henry and Emily Sloane Hammond House**
(Now Consulate General of the Russian Federation in

New York), 9 East 91st Street (Carrère & Hastings, 1902-03). In 1901, William and Emily Vanderbilt Sloane purchased a 137-foot wide midblock site from Andrew Carnegie with the intention of building houses for their two daughters. Florence Sloane and her husband, James A. Burden, the son of the founder of the Burden Ironworks in Troy, moved into one of the largest Beaux-Arts townhouses in New York. The street elevation has a striking sculptural quality evident at the concave windows of the main story and in the heavy raised banding of the two lower floors. Vehicles could enter the house through the arch that pierces the ground floor of the front elevation; they exited through a wide opening into the side court. The Sloanes provided their daughter Emily and son-in-law, lawyer John Henry Hammond, with a well-proportioned limestone mansion inspired by the architecture of the Italian Renaissance.

Florence Burden sold No. 7 in 1938 and a year later it became part of the Convent of the Sacred Heart School. The Hammonds retained their property until 1946 when they moved into an apartment on Park Avenue (Hammond died three years later while preparing to putt on the tenth green of the U.S. Seniors' Golf Tournament at the Apawanis Club in Rye, N.Y.). In 1975, the house became the Soviet consulate. Following the invasion of Afghanistan in 1979, the consulate was closed and the building remained vacant until 1993 when it was reoccupied and the deterioration caused by the closure was repaired.

CH15 Spence School

20 East 91st Street (John Russell Pope, 1929). American classicist John Russell Pope was commissioned to design a new home for the Spence School, a fashionable private institution for young women founded in 1892 by Clara B. Spence. Spence had been located in Midtown, but chose to move to Carnegie Hill because its old locale was becoming increasingly commercial and most of its students resided on the Upper East Side. Pope created a subtle Colonial Revival structure that resembles, in design

and scale, many of the apartment houses erected on the side streets between Fifth and Park avenues during the 1920s. The contextual two-story west wing was designed in 1987 by Fox & Fowle.

Walk to the corner of Madison Avenue and turn left.

1285-1293 Madison Avenue, 1889

CH16 1285-1293 Madison Avenue
Southeast corner East 92nd Street (James E. Ware, 1889-90). These five Romanesque Revival dwellings were among the last speculative rowhouses erected on Madison Avenue and are an indication that this street was once popular for middle-class residences. Not until early

in the 20th century were the single-family homes converted for commercial use. For this row, James E. Ware created a lively facade of contrasting red brick and brownstone. A surprisingly large number of original details survive despite the commercial alterations. Note, for example, the three original entrance arches, the small square window panes at Nos. 1285 and 1289, and the roofline parapet with its recessed brick panels.

CH17 William Goadby and Florence Baker Loew House

Continue north on Madison to East 93rd Street. Turn right.

(Now Smithers Alcoholism Center), 56 East 93rd Street (Walker & Gillette, 1930-31). Stockbroker and socialite William Loew and his wife undoubtedly chose to build their home on this site because Florence Loew's brother, James Baker, Jr., lived across the street (CH19). The English Regency-inspired building is one of the last great townhouses erected in Manhattan. Its striking design elements include a two-story concave street front, subtly complex pattern of windows, and set back upper stories that create the illusion of a low building. Especially fine features include the fan-like arches on the second story, the carved curtains that grace the central third-story window, and the iron railings with lamps.

CH18 Virginia Graham Fair Vanderbilt House

(Now Lycée Français de New-York), 60 East 93rd Street (John Russell Pope, 1930-31). John Russell Pope, best known as the architect of the National Gallery in Washington, was also an important designer of traditional city houses. For heiress Virginia Vanderbilt, the divorced wife of William K. Vanderbilt, Jr. and the daughter of James Fair whose fortune came from mining the Nevada Comstock Lode, Pope provided an imposing rendition of a French townhouse from the era of Louis XV. The simplicity of the street front, with its balanced proportions and modest ornamental flourishes — note the keystones in the form of women's heads and the magnificent carved oak doors — typifies 20th-century adaptations of 18th-century design.

Continue east on East 93rd Street.

Baker House complex,
c.1930

CH19 James F. Baker, Jr. House Complex

(Now partly Russian Orthodox Church Outside Russia),
67, 69, and 75 East 93rd Street, northwest corner Park
Avenue (Delano & Aldrich: main house, 1917-18; ball-
room wing, 1928; No. 69, 1928-29; No. 67, 1931).
The handsome brick and marble corner house at No. 75
East 93rd Street was designed for financier Francis F.
Palmer by the firm of Delano & Aldrich in the restrained
Neo-classical style that was its specialty. A decade after
construction began the house was sold to James F. Baker,
Jr., then vice-president of the First National Bank (now
Citibank), and his wife, Edith. For the Bakers, Delano &
Aldrich designed a series of additions, all of which har-
monize with the original work. The ballroom wing to
the west and the two-story garage at No. 69 form a spacious courtyard. The garage features the boldest architectural element of the complex, a colonnade of paired,
fluted marble Ionic columns. Farther west, at No. 67,
Baker demolished a brownstone rowhouse (visible in
the photograph), in order to build a house for his father,
James Baker, Sr., the main force behind the creation of
First National Bank, but he died before its completion; at
the senior Baker's death "young Mr. Baker," as James, Jr.
was known for most of his life, inherited $60 million
and became chairman of the board of the bank. The nau-

tical motifs that ornament each addition — a conch shell at the ballroom, scallop shells at the garage, and a pair of dolphins at No. 67 — may be associated with Baker's yachting interests; in fact, he died on his yacht Viking in 1937. The main house and ballroom wing have been the Russian Orthodox Church Outside Russia since 1958.

CH20 1185 Park Avenue

East side between 93rd and 94th streets (Schwartz & Gross, 1928-29). Encompassing an entire blockfront on Park Avenue, this is the only Upper East Side apartment building designed with the interior courtyard plan used at such prominent Upper West Side buildings as the Dakota, Apthorp, and Belnord. Schwartz & Gross created a brick building with Gothic-inspired limestone and terra-cotta detail. An ornate portal at the center of the Park Avenue elevation frames the vaulted entrance drive, with its ornate plaster and cast-stone detail. The drive leads into the landscaped courtyard where access is gained to the apartments (there were originally 173) via six separate entrances.

CH21 East 95th Street between Park and Lexington Avenues

Nos. 115-127 (Louis Entzer, Jr., 1891-92); Nos. 129-143 (Frank Wennemer, 1889-90); Nos. 112-114 and 1213-1217 Park Avenue (Flemer & Koehler, 1889-90); Nos. 116-138, (C. Abbott French & Co., 1887-88). The small, fanciful rowhouses on this somewhat out-of-the-way block create one of the most charming residential enclaves in New York. Although local legend has it that these houses were built for workers in the nearby Ruppert Brewery, they were actually erected by three specu-lative builders who undoubtedly believed that this loca-tion near the Third Avenue El was a prime site for houses that could be sold to middle-class families. The brick and stone houses were designed in the Romanesque Revival and Queen Anne styles by four obscure firms. Their richly textured facades, many still retaining straight or L-shaped stoops, are filled with superb details. A careful examination will be well rewarded — note for example,

Walk to corner of East 93rd Street and Park Avenue.

Cross Park Avenue and turn left. Peer through the entrance arch of No. 1185. You are now at the crest of Carnegie Hill; note how the avenue slopes as you walk north to East 95th Street. Turn right.

Reverse direction and walk back to Park Avenue. Cross Park and continue west (outside of the historic district) to Madison passing the mock-castle wall of the Squadron A Armory (John R. Thomas, 1893-95; an individual landmark). Cross Madison (reentering the historic district) and turn right. Turn left on East 96th Street.

the varied projecting oriels, the quirky rooflines, the multi-paneled doors (some with original mailbox slots and doorknobs), and the imaginative stone and terracotta ornament that includes human and satyr heads, monsters, and a panoply of foliate detail.

CH22a Lucy Dahlgren House
15 East 96th Street (1915-16); **CH22b Ogden Codman House** (now Manhattan Country School, 7 East 96th Street (1912-13); **CH22c Robert L. and Marie Livingston House** (now Scuola New York Guglielmo Marconi), 12 East 96th Street (1916-17); all designed by Ogden Codman. In 1908, Ogden Codman purchased the lot at 7 East 96th Street from Andrew Carnegie with the intention of building a house for his own use that would also serve as an advertisement for his sophisticated design aesthetic. Although Codman is best known as an interior decorator (he and Edith Wharton wrote

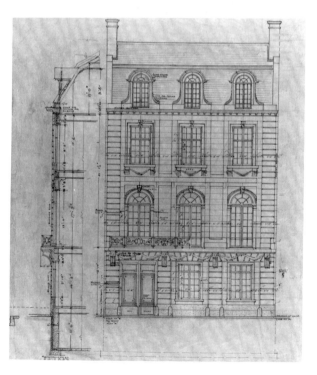

Ogden Codman's 1912 design for his own house

94

The Decoration of Houses, a landmark examination of this subject), he was also responsible for a number of superb New York townhouses. Codman's townhouse was the first of a row of four that he conceived for the north side of 96th Street; only his house and the Dahlgren House at No. 15 were built. The Codman and Dahlgren houses, and the smaller Livingston House across the street, illustrate Codman's love of 18th-century French residential architecture. Neither Codman nor Dahlgren lived on 96th Street for long. By 1920, Codman's practice had declined and he retired to France. Heiress Lucy Drexel Dahlgren spent little time in her house and by 1922 it was the home of jeweler Pierre Cartier.

Walk to Fifth Avenue and turn left. Continue south, past several apartment houses dating from 1921-22, to 95th Street. Turn left.

CH23 Mrs. Amory B. Carhart House

(Now Lycée Français de New-York), 3 East 95th Street (Horace Trumbauer, 1913-16). The year after completion of the Duke House at Fifth Avenue and 78th Street (MM3), Horace Trumbauer received the commission for this large house from the recently widowed Mrs. Carhart. The design, inspired by the late 18th-century French townhouses built during the reign of Louis XVI, is representative of the work coming from Trumbauer's office in Philadelphia, under the leadership of black architect Julian Abele, Trumbauer's chief draftsman. The limestone facade is enlivened with exquisitely crafted ornament: keystones in the form of heads; a delicate iron balcony railing with openwork urns; and allegorical relief panels representing war and peace and commerce and abundance. Mrs. Carhart lived here only briefly before her death in 1918.

CH24 Ernesto and Edith Fabbri House

(Now House of the Redeemer), 7 East 95th Street (attributed to Egisto Fabbri with Grosvenor Atterbury, 1914-16). In 1900, shortly after their marriage, Italian Count Ernesto Fabbri and the former Edith Shepard moved into a large Beaux-Arts townhouse at 11 East 62nd Street (UES6). In 1916, the Fabbris completed a new residence designed to resemble an Italian Renaissance palace. Evidence suggests that Count Fabbri's brother, the Italian architect and interior designer Egisto Fabbri, was responsible for the design, with local architect Grosvenor Atterbury assisting. The L-shaped brick and stone house contains a small courtyard guarded by an iron railing which displays the Fabbri coat of arms — an arm holding a hammer. The interior was decorated with Italian Renaissance antiques, including an entire room thought to have been relocated from the Ducal Palace in Urbino. Mrs. Fabbri transferred the property to the House of the Redeemer, an Episcopal retreat center, in 1949.

Return to Fifth Avenue and turn left. Walk to the southeast corner of Fifth Avenue and 94th Street.

CH25 Willard and Dorothy Whitney Straight House

(Now International Center of Photography), 1130 Fifth Avenue, northeast corner East 94th Street (Delano & Aldrich, 1913-15). Although only 38 at his death in 1918, Willard Straight was one of the country's most prominent financiers and diplomats, and, in association with his wife, the founder of The New Republic. For the Straights, Delano & Aldrich provided one of its boldest designs; one inspired in large part by Sir Christopher Wren's late 17th-century wing at Hampton Court Palace near London (this is especially evident in the use of round windows). The Baroque quality of Wren's building was tempered by the flat, refined Neo-classical forms that are Delano & Aldrich's hallmark. Especially lovely details are the wrought-iron peacock set above the entrance and the carved birds pecking at a bowl of fruit in the frieze of the central second-story window. The building is now a museum; the main hall, with its black and white marble floor and Adamesque ceiling embellished with painted rondels, is worth a visit.

Turn left on East 94th Street.

CH26 East 94th Street between Fifth and Madison Avenues.

Speculative rowhouse development swept through the park blocks south of East 96th Street in the last decade of the 19th century. The 94th Street blockfronts, which have undergone relatively little alteration, are representative of the substantial houses that developers built in order to attract upper middle-class buyers to the neighborhood. The brownstone and limestone Romanesque Revival dwellings at Nos. 5-25 (Cleverdon & Putzel, 1892-94), with their rough stone and Byzantine carving, were among the last rowhouses in Manhattan erected with high stoops (two L-shaped stoops survive) and raised basements. By 1900 rowhouses designed in the so-called American basement plan, identified by a main entrance at or close to street level and a service entrance set to one side, had become popular. This can be seen at the limestone and brick Beaux-Arts row at Nos. 18-24 (Van Vleck & Goldsmith, 1899-1900). Most of the rowhouses on the street were owned by affluent merchants and manufacturers, many of whom were immigrants from German-speaking areas of Central Europe. Although these are relatively large dwellings, most were occupied by large households; several families had six children and up to six servants (most of the servants were also German speaking, although the owner of No. 24 employed a Chinese chef — a rare instance of a live-in Asian servant in New York).

CH27 Felix and Frieda Warburg House

(Now Jewish Museum), 1109 Fifth Avenue, northeast corner East 92nd Street (C.P.H. Gilbert, 1907-09). Apparently, Felix and Frieda Warburg, prominent members of New York's German-Jewish aristocracy, were so impressed with the François I style châteaux that C.P.H. Gilbert had designed for the Fletchers (MM8) and Woolworths (MM10) farther south on Fifth Avenue, that they commissioned a similar house for themselves. For the Warburgs, Gilbert created a house that, in its basic form, is similar to the Fletchers', but is somewhat more refined. The Warburg House is more artfully massed, with a subtle balance of window and door openings and projecting and receding planes, but it is less whimsical than the earlier dwelling, lacking much of the droll detail that so enlivens the 79th Street house.

In 1944, Frieda Warburg donated the house to the Jewish Theological Seminary which converted it into a museum. In 1988 Kevin Roche, John Dinkerloo & Asso-

Return to Fifth Avenue and turn left. Walk past a series of limestone and brick apartment houses from 1924-26 to the corner of Fifth Avenue and 92nd Street.

Warburg House in 1925

ciates was commissioned to design an extension on Fifth Avenue. Rather than designing a creative contemporary structure, the firm imitated Gilbert's design. The character of the early 20th-century carved limestone detail was expertly replicated, but the balance and integrity of the original mansion have been compromised.

CH28 1107 Fifth Avenue

Southeast corner East 92nd Street (Rouse & Goldstone, 1924-25). In the years following World War I, as land values rose and as lifestyles changed, many wealthy New Yorkers found maintaining a private house to be too costly or inconvenient. One of these was Marjorie Merriweather Post Hutton, heir to the Post cereal fortune and wife of financier E.F. Hutton. Mrs. Hutton sold her home on this corner to an apartment house developer, with the proviso that he create a triplex apartment for her exclusive use. The apartment, on the top two floors and penthouse, is clearly demarcated by tall rectangular windows, a limestone beltcourse with window balustrades, corner terraces, and a large Palladian window that once lit Mrs. Hutton's foyer. While other residents entered the building on Fifth Avenue, the Huttons and their guests used an entrance set beneath the porte cochère on 92nd Street that led to a private elevator. The apartment, said to have been the largest ever created in New York, has been subdivided.

1107 Fifth Avenue in 1925

Tour IV: The Treadwell Farm Historic District

Introduction

The small Treadwell Farm Historic District, encompassing East 61st and 62nd streets between Second and Third avenues, was one of the Landmark Preservation Commission's earliest historic district designations, dating from 1967. The district was named for the Treadwell family which owned the undeveloped land in this area from 1815 through the late 1860s when residential construction began. Most of the buildings in the historic district are four-story rowhouses, originally erected between 1868 and 1875. The Commission designated these buildings because of the special ambiance of these streets, nestled between two busy avenues.

In the years since the designation, many people have been puzzled by the Commission's action since most of the houses have been altered. The difficulty with this designation arises from the fact that it has been analyzed as a district primarily composed of brownstone-fronted rowhouses from the post-Civil War period. This is not what the district is really all about, nor is it what makes these two streets so interesting. These streets should be valued largely as examples of the design aesthetic of the late 1910s and 1920s, an era when major changes were occurring to New York's aging rowhouses. In fact, in the years immediately after World War I, almost every house in the Treadwell Farm Historic District was changed. Many of the rowhouses were stripped of projecting details and redesigned in a simplified mode with subtle ornamental flourishes.

The route of this tour is quite simple. Start on East 61st Street, just east of Third Avenue; walk east on 61st Street; turn left on Second Avenue and walk to East 62nd Street; turn left onto 62nd Street; walk west toward Third Avenue.

Tour

TF1 206-210 East 61st Street
(Frederick S. Barus, 1873-75). This is an appropriate

place to start the Treadwell Farm tour, since these three late Italianate brownstone-fronted houses, survivors from a row of five, are among the few in the historic district that retain most of their original features, including high stoops, entrances flanked by Tuscan columns, sculptural window frames, projecting metal cornices, and unusual paired round-arched windows on each parlor story. The only important changes are the addition of the multi-paned windows at No. 206, added in 1920 by architect Josephine Wright Chapman, and the loss of the stoop at No. 208.

TF2 205-209 East 61st Street
(Breen & Nason, architect/builder, 1873-74) and **211-221 East 61st Street** (Alfred & Samuel Bussell, architect/builder, 1875). A glance along the north side of this street readily reveals the contrast between the intact 19th-century houses, such as No. 209, with its stoop and three-dimensional carved ornament, and the flatter, more streamlined designs of those houses altered in the 20th century. Note the subtle detail on the redesigned houses: the brick basement at No. 205, the pedimented Neo-Georgian entrance and ornate window decoration at No. 207, the projecting oriel and iron balconies at No. 211, the iron fence and lamp at No. 213, and the Greek fret and raised parapet panels at No. 217. Curiously, not every original detail was removed from every redesigned house; for example, several retain bracketed Neo-Grec cornices.

TF3 216 East 61st Street
(Frederick S. Barus, 1870; redesign, Nelson K. Vanderbeek, 1921-22). This house is one of several in the district that received touches of medieval-inspired ornament during the process of facade redesign. Note the wonderful leaded transom with its colored-glass unicorn set above the entrance door.

TF4 224 East 61st Street
(Frederick S. Barus, 1871; redesign, Josephine Wright Chapman, 1919). Josephine Wright Chapman was one of the few women to maintain a successful architectural practice in the United States during the early years of the 20th century. She designed a number of suburban houses in the New York City

area as well as several rowhouse alterations. At 224 East 61st Street, realtor Richard L. Beckwith had Chapman convert what had become a two-family house back into a single-family residence for his own use. She planned interior changes and, on the exterior, removed the stoop and projecting exterior ornament. It was apparently Chapman who was responsible for the multi-paned window sash and the magnificent Neo-medieval wooden door with its iron knocker.

TF5 223 East 61st Street

(Jacob M. Felson, 1941-42). In 1941 Jacob Felson was commissioned to replace the 61st Street Methodist Episcopal Church (John Welch, 1873-75) with a new apartment building. This red brick structure typifies the Colonial Revival as it was adapted for middle-class apartment house design. However, it contains a few distinguishing features, notably the metal casement windows, the cast-stone swan's-neck entrance pediment capped by a stylized pineapple (a traditional symbol of hospitality), the quaint shutters with sailboat cutouts, and the cast-stone pineapples and whimsical chimney pots at the roofline.

TF6 232 East 61st Street

(Frederick S. Barus, 1873; redesign, John William Tumbridge, 1922-23). Extensive remodeling of this house entailed the removal of all exterior detail and the addition of a full story. The focal point of the design is the ground-floor entrance with its delicate Doric frieze and carved fan.

TF7 234 East 61st Street

(Frederick S. Barus, 1873; redesign, Raymond Hood, 1919-20). This rather traditional redesign project was an early work by Raymond Hood, the architect who, a few years later, would pioneer in the design of modern skyscrapers and apartment buildings (see MM21). Although Hood removed the stoop and stripped all projecting detail, there is little evidence of his design skill; the main entrance door and its flanking lamps and the translucent

Rear facade of 234 East 61st Street

bottle glass in the central window and eastern door may
be Hood's work. At the rear, Hood added a two-story
addition with a Spanish Baroque flavor.

*First Swedish Baptist
Church, with frescoes
by Olle Nordmark,
c. 1929*

TF8 First Swedish Baptist Church

(Now Trinity Baptist Church), 250 East 61st Street (Martin Hedmark, 1929). New York's ethnic communities
have often erected singular buildings that reflect the
design heritage of their native lands. This spectacular
Baptist church designed for a Swedish congregation by
an architect who had only recently emigrated from Swe-
den is a superb example. The church is a modern adaptation of vernacular Swedish ecclesiastical design. The tall
street wall crowned by a stepped gable is a feature found
on buildings in the Baltic Sea region, and the towers with
their metal caps are versions of the wooden steeples of
Swedish churches. The use of brick is extraordinary, with
four shades graded from brown at the base to a lighter
buff in the gable, and complex patterns at the round
windows. The flat hand-hammered metalwork, including iron bands on the doors, the "angel forest" above the
central door, and the stylized figures of Adam, Eve, and
the angel Gabriel at the service entrance to the west, is
unmatched in New York. The spectacular use of materials continues on the interior, as is evident in the accom-

panying photograph. The First Swedish Baptist Church was founded in 1867, but as the Swedish-speaking population in New York City declined, English was adopted for services and in 1942 the name of the congregation was changed to Trinity Baptist. A restoration of the church was begun in 1991.

249 East 61st Street (right) in 1939

TF9 249 East 61st Street

(Florentine Pelletier, 1868-69; redesign, Sterner & Wolfe, 1919-20). Frederick Sterner was a pioneer in the redesign of rowhouse facades in the early decades of the 20th century and was also one of the most talented architects involved with this development. This narrow house is the most sophisticated in the district. As was typical of Sterner's work, he had most of the projecting elements of the original brownstone front removed. He then covered the front with a light-colored stucco that is in marked contrast to the original somber brownstone design, evident at no. 247 and seen to the left in the accompanying photograph. Sterner generally added subtle artistic details to his rowhouse facades; here, these include the header bricks that outline the ground-floor entrance and windows, the five small attached plaques, and the iron balconies and fence.

Walk to East 62nd Street.

TF10 245 and 247 East 62nd Street

(George F. Pelham, 1899-1900). This pair of "old-law" tenements was erected at a time when the neighborhood was attracting large numbers of working-class immigrants. Although the exterior is well-proportioned and features handsome stone and terra-cotta ornament, these are examples of the worst type of housing erected in New York during the final years of the 19th century. Each is a six-story walk-up that housed 24 families — four per floor — with one hall toilet for every two families. They are late examples of the dumbbell tenement (a form outlawed in 1901), so named because, in plan, their small light courts create a shape that resembles a dumbbell weight. According to 1905 census records, the buildings housed working people, many of whom were immigrants from Central Europe.

TF11 Presbyterian Church of the Redeemer

(Now Our Lady of Peace R.C. Church), 239 East 62nd Street (Samuel A. Warner, 1886-87). The German-speaking congregation of the Church of the Redeemer

Presbyterian Church of the Redeemer with 229-231 East 62nd Street (TF14) at left, c.1905

105

was organized in 1885 and one year later erected this church in an area with an increasingly large German population. The congregation remained until 1899 when it merged with another German-language church. The church is a symmetrical Victorian Gothic brick building with stone and terra-cotta trim.

TF12 234 East 62nd Street

(James W. Pirsson, 1868-69; redesign, LaFarge, Warren & Clark, 1930). In 1930, the Italianate row house on this lot was redesigned as a home for architect Christopher Grant LaFarge and his wife, Louisa, by LaFarge's firm. Although some remodeling had occurred here in 1921, it appears that the most significant changes, the removal of the stoop and construction of a basement entrance with elegant doorways flanking attenuated paired pilasters, date from this later alteration.

TF13 230 East 62nd Street

(James W. Pirsson, 1868-69; redesign, Aymar Embury II, 1927). Architect Aymar Embury created one of the most refined redesign schemes in the district for the facade of his own home. Embury, who is best remembered for his Depression-era park projects undertaken for Robert Moses, including the original buildings at the Central Park Zoo, had established his career during the 1920s as an architect of traditionally-styled houses (UES 36a, 36c). On 62nd Street, Embury stripped all of the detail from the facade of a brownstone house, save its rusticated base. A new stucco front was applied, highlighted by such elegant Neo-classical features as large rosettes and keystones in the form of covered bowls. In front of the house is a Greek Revival iron railing, probably cast in the late 1830s. During the 1920s, when many early rowhouses in Greenwich Village, Chelsea, and other neighborhoods were being demolished for new buildings, historic features such as doorways, mantels, and ironwork were often salvaged and incorporated into new buildings. Embury apparently purchased this old railing as the perfect accessory for his new home.

TF14 219-225 East 62nd Street

(Richard Morris Hunt, 1873-74) and **227-231 East 62nd Street** (Duncan J. MacRae, 1874-75). These seven unusual Neo-Grec houses originally appeared as a single unified row(see photo, page 105). Because they were built on exceptionally shallow lots, the houses have no front yards, but extend forward to the lot line. All seven were erected by the speculative builders Thomas and John Crimmins. Richard Morris Hunt, who was only just establishing himself as a leading figure among New York's architects in 1873, designed the four houses to the west, using the stylized French-inspired detail with which he had become familiar while studying at the Ecole des Beaux-Arts in Paris. Four months after Hunt's houses were completed, the builders applied to extend the row to the east and hired an obscure architect named Duncan MacRae. MacRae simply copied Hunt's earlier design. It is one of MacRae's houses, No. 227, that retains the most original features, including recessed spandrels set between the second and third floors, oddly-shaped lintels, and a cornice with unusual raised panels.

TF15 222 East 62nd Street

(J. and G. Ruddell, 1868). The contrast between the character of the original rowhouses in the Treadwell Farm Historic District and the remodeled facades is graphically illustrated by comparing this intact mid-19th-century residence with nearby houses redesigned after World War I. No. 222 retains its brownstone front, high stoop, three-dimensional window frames, bracketed cornice, double-hung wooden window sash, and double doors, all features stripped from most of the other houses in the district.

TF16 218 East 62nd Street

(Frederick S. Barus, 1870; redesign, Kahn & Jacobs, 1940). The last major change to occur in the historic district was the addition of a Modern facade to this house. Ely Jacques Kahn, who is best known for his Art Deco skyscrapers, replaced the original brownstone with a simple, yet carefully balanced brick front with no applied ornament. The red brick facade, enlivened by randomly-placed burned bricks, is articulated by metal casement windows set in horizontal strips, a feature Kahn borrowed from progressive European architecture. Although a garage was incorporated into the 1940 alteration, the present granite cladding of the lower story is a later addition.

TF17 211 East 62nd Street

(Mortimer C. Merritt, 1872-73; new facade, William C. Lauritzen, 1925-26). This house is the only one in the historic district in which the original front was completely removed and a totally new front constructed at the lot line. The new facade is clad entirely in textured brick laid in Flemish bond and is articulated by casement windows with colored glass panes. Simple ornamental highlights include limestone entrance enframements and an iron balcony.

211 East 62nd Street in 1939

Tour V: The Henderson Place Historic District

Introduction

The Henderson Place Historic District, designated a landmark in 1969, is one of New York City's most remarkable residential enclaves. This cluster of 24 small Queen Anne dwellings, surviving from an original group of 32, was built in 1881-82 for "persons of moderate means." The enclave was the creation of John C. Henderson, a prosperous fur importer and fur-hat dealer who also invested in New York City real estate. Henderson purchased the property on East 86th and 87th streets and East End Avenue between 1855 and 1857. He held it for about 25 years before building. In 1881, at age 72, Henderson finally began construction on the site. Rather than building in the traditional New York manner, with all houses facing onto public streets, Henderson laid out a new street, named for himself, and arranged many of the small residences along this cul-de-sac. Designed by Lamb & Rich, the houses range from 14 to 20 feet wide (most are 17 or 18 feet wide) and are three stories tall with sunken basements. As is vividly illustrated here, the architects were among the most talented interpreters of the Queen Anne style in New York. The Henderson Place houses show how a creative use of Queen Anne details can transform a group of modest dwellings into a joyous architectural statement. Wide arched entryways, terracotta plaques, windows divided into tiny square panes, projecting bays and oriels, twisting iron railings, and slate-covered mansard roofs with projecting dormers, gables, chimneys, and towerlettes all contribute to the architectural novelty of the homes.

Unlike most New York developers who hoped to quickly sell their rowhouses at maximum profit, Henderson planned to profit from renting his buildings. While each house is small, most were leased to fairly large households, some with as many of seven or eight

Henderson Place in 1937

people, including a significant number of female servants (from their surnames, most appear to have been Irish). Most residents were relatively young — not one person over the age of 50 lived here in 1890. Although there were several households headed by women, most were headed by business and professional men, including those involved in insurance, grain, rags, skins, and cutlery, as well as one well-known architect, Charles Palliser who lived at 556 East 87th Street (Palliser published several books of house designs and plans).

In 1889, following John Henderson's death, the houses were divided among twelve heirs; each received two or three units. Two years later, the first house left Henderson-family ownership, but most were not sold by Henderson's heirs until the 20th century. Prior to designation of the historic district several of the houses underwent alterations, including the construction of additional stories, which marred portions of the picturesque roofline. The most unfortunate change occurred in 1960 when the eight houses on the west side of Henderson Place were replaced by a banal apartment house that is out of scale with the diminutive homes.

Tour

HP1 Henderson Place

The five houses on the east side of Henderson Place form the best preserved blockfront in the historic district. Although not apparent at first glance, this is a symmetrical row centering on No. 12 with its large pedimented gable. The flanking houses feature rooflines articulated by pairs of dormers, all of which are capped by round-arch pediments (Nos. 8 and 14 retain original carved wooden fans) except for the curious house at No. 16 with its triangular pediments. The facades are decorated with classical forms used in an ornamental and highly unorthodox fashion. These houses clearly illustrate why the English architects who devised the Queen Anne style originally referred to it as "Free Classic." Notice, for example, the classically-inspired stone moldings that

Since Henderson Place is a small and cohesive unit, the tour will provide a discussion of some of the more interesting features of each of the four blockfronts in the district. Start on Henderson Place.

rest on the keystones of the parlor-story windows, the carved panels below the parlor window sills, and the terra-cotta swags on the second story.

HP2 East 86th Street

The 86th Street houses are the narrowest in the district — averaging only 16 feet in width. The size precluded the use of grand stoops, yet each stoop gracefully curves or angles up from the sidewalk to a parlor-level entrance. A steep stair leads down to a secondary basement entrance. As is typical of Queen Anne dwellings, unexpected details enliven the facades: for example, the two-story oriel that serves as a transitional element on the house at the corner of Henderson Place; the tall brick chimney ornamented with terra-cotta blocks between Nos. 551 and 553; the galvanized-iron dormers with randomly-placed rosettes and rondels; and the superb brick corbelling (26-courses tall) at the entrance to No. 553.

HP3 East End Avenue

Although the houses on this street have undergone the most alteration, especially at the roofline, the block still retains much of its fanciful Queen Anne character. The windows at No. 142 provide a good example of the multi-paned sash with small square panes once found on many Queen Anne buildings. The red brick facades are relieved by stone and terra-cotta details carefully placed to add interest to the row. The roofline of the central houses, Nos. 148 and 150, is especially fine, with its towerlettes and the quirky roof slopes and finials that survive at No. 148. A similar roof caps the tower that serves as a transition between the houses on East End Avenue and those on East 87th Street.

HP4 East 87th Street

The contrast between smooth and rough textured materials emblematic of Queen Anne design is especially evident on this blockfront, as is the exploitation of small window panes, adding a lively pattern to the facades — at No. 552 the upper sash on the second floor has 32

small panes! Other wonderful features are the wide arched entrance with elongated stone keystone at No. 556, the dormers at Nos. 552 and 554, the original multi-paneled wooden doors, and the twisted iron railings.

East End Avenue and East 87th Street in 1892

Local Resources

For information on how you can assist in the preservation of the Upper East Side's landmark buildings and historic districts, or for more information about local preservation efforts, you can contact the following preservation organizations:

Friends of the Upper East Side Historic Districts
20 East 69th Street
New York, NY 10021
535-2526

Carnegie Hill Neighbors
80 East 96th Street
New York, NY 10128
996-5520

Historic Districts Council
45 West 67th Street
New York, NY 10023
496-8110

New York City Landmarks Preservation Commission
100 Old Slip
New York, NY 10005
487-6700

New York Landmarks Conservancy
141 Fifth Avenue
New York, NY 10010
995-5260

Selected Bibliography

Boyer, M. Christine. *Manhattan Manners: Architecture and Style 1850-1900*. NY: Rizzoli, 1985.

Cromley, Elizabeth Collins. *Alone Together: A History of New York's Early Apartments*. Ithaca: Cornell University Press, 1990.

"The Contemporary Metropolitan Residence," *Real Estate Record and Builders Guide* 73 (June 11, 1904) 1447-62.

Croly, Herbert, "The Renovation of the New York Brownstone District," *Architectural Record* 63 (June 1903) 555-71.

Dolkart, Andrew S. *The Landmark Commission's Guide to New York City Landmarks* Washington: Preservation Press and New York: Landmarks Preservation Commission, 1992.

History of Real Estate, Building and Architecture in New York City During the Last Quarter of a Century. NY: Record and Guide, 1896; reprint ed, NY: Arno, 1967.

Lockwood, Charles. *Bricks and Brownstone*. NY: McGraw-Hill, 1972.

New York City Landmarks Preservation Commission.
Expanded Carnegie Hill Historic District Designation Report (1993).
Henderson Place Historic District Designation Report (1969).
Metropolitan Museum of Art Historic District Designation Report (1977).
Treadwell Farm Historic District Designation Report (1967).
Upper East Side Historic District Designation Report, ed. Marjorie Pearson (1981).

"Review of Progress on the East Side," *Real Estate Record and Builders Guide* 47 (May 30, 1891), supplement.

Schuyler, Montgomery, "The New New York House," *Architectural Record* 19 (Feb. 1906) 83-103.

Schuyler, Montgomery, [Franz K. Winkler], "Architecture in the Billionaire District of New York City," *Architectural Record* 11 (October 1901) 681-699.

Stern, Robert A.M. et al. *New York 1900*. NY: Rizzoli, 1983.

Stern, Robert A.M. et al. *New York 1930*. NY: Rizzoli, 1987.

Trager, James. *Park Avenue: Street of Dreams*. NY: Atheneum, 1990.

White, Norval and Elliott Willensky. *AIA Guide to New York City*. 3rd ed. NY: Harcourt Brace Jovanovich, 1988.

Architects and Artists Index

Buildings Index

(Buildings indexed by original name and present name; where no specific name is applicable, the address is listed).

Illustration Sources

The New York Landmarks Conservancy greatly appreciates the opportunity to reproduce illustrations from the following collections and institutions.

Archives and Libraries

Avery Architectural and Fine Arts Library, Division of Drawings and Archives, Columbia University in the City of New York; Delano & Aldrich Collection p.78; McKim, Mead & White Collection pp.61, 92; Ogden Codman Collection p.94

Bank of New York Museum: p.36

City of New York Department of Records and Information Services, Municipal Archives: pp.104, 108

Collection of The New-York Historical Society: pp.75, 110

Library of Congress: pp.12, 14, 46, 51, 62, 71, 83, 90, 103

The Museum of the City of New York: pp.27, 29, 38, 42, 52, 86, 99, 113

Syracuse University Archives, Lescaze Collection: p.56

The New York Public Library, Astor, Lenox and Tilden Foundations, United States History, Local History and Genealogy Division: pp. 9, 15, 98, 105

UPI Bettman Archive: p.16

Publications

Architect: p.30 (May 1929)

Architectural Record: p.73 (October 1901), p.48 (March 1922), p.67 (October 1901), p.88 (August 1919)

Architectural Yearbook: p.41 (1912), p.81 (1925), p.85 (1927), p.39 (1939)

Architecture: p.32 (April 1916), p.59 (March 1909)

Architecture and Building: p. 103 (February 1931)

Monograph of the Works of McKim, Mead & White (1915): pp. 54, 64

New York Architect: p.69 (March 1912)

Pease & Elliman's Book of Apartment House Plans (1922): pp.33, 68, 80

The Real Estate Record And Builders Guide: p.10 (April 2, 1892), p.79 (January 28, 1911), pp.83, 90 (May 30, 1891)